WOMEN AND GUILT

WOMEN AND GUILT

*How to
set aside your
feelings of guilt
and lead a
positive life*

URSULA MARKHAM

PIATKUS

*A catalogue record for this book is available
from the British Library*

ISBN 0-7499-1442-4

Edited by Maggie Daykin
Designed by Sue Ryall
Typeset by Computerset Ltd, Harmondsworth
Printed and bound in Great Britain by
Butler & Tanner Ltd, Frome, Somerset

To the women who have meant so much to me:
my mother, my grandmother and my special friends

'Beauty is eternity gazing at itself in a mirror.
But you are eternity and you are the mirror.'
(KAHLIL GIBRAN, *The Prophet*)

Contents

Introduction

Guilt can be a terrible and often crippling emotion. It is not by chance that we have coined such phrases as being 'consumed by guilt', or 'eaten up with guilt'. Excessive guilt which is not properly handled can indeed 'eat away' at us, causing physical, mental and emotional illness.

Naturally, everyone is capable of experiencing guilt to a greater or lesser degree, and you may wonder therefore why I am singling out women for special attention. I am doing so because women are certainly the world champions! I am not belittling men, nor am I denying their sensitivity or their regret for past wrongs. In current times, however, it is women who are by far the greater sufferers from this destructive emotion – see especially Chapter Three, which concentrates on why this is so.

Whether they are suffering because of past wrongs, are being manipulated by others in the present or doubt their ability to make good decisions about the future, many women live for years in a state of perpetual guilt from which they are usually only able to escape by means of help from outside professionals. In the course of this book, however, I hope to show you how you can deal with the problem yourself, and break free of the legacy of harmful experiences in the past, thus allowing yourself to live in a positive way: giving the most to life while getting the most from it.

The topics I cover include understanding:

- how destructive guilt can be and the harm it can do both physically as well as emotionally

- why it is that women seem to suffer from extreme guilt more than men do

- the importance of developing a positive self-image and learning to like yourself

- how to deal with situations where you have been in the wrong

- how to avoid manipulation by other people

- how to deal with negative family relationships (past and present)

- how guilt can be induced by sexual stresses

- how to cope with bereavement

At all stages you will not only be given details of case histories (with names changed, of course) taken from my files, but also self-help techniques to help you rid yourself of any harmful and unnecessary guilt.

Ursula Markham, October 1994

— 1 —

The Destructive
Power
of Guilt

We all have things which make us feel guilty. For one person it may be eating a chocolate bar when she is supposed to be on a diet. For another it may be a past misdemeanour which she has not been able to erase from her memory.

You may find it comparatively easy to get over the guilt pangs which arise from eating the chocolate bar – although if you are a long-term 'failed' slimmer, this may not be so. Managing to put behind you, once and for all, a genuine crime or misdemeanour committed in the past will almost certainly be difficult. In fact, you may feel that you should not be allowed to do so, particularly if real harm has been done to another person.

The question is: does living with that guilt make you a better person? Are you any happier because you constantly remind yourself of something you regret doing? I doubt it. Of course, in consequence you may have *chosen* to become a better person. And that *is* commendable. But it is even more commendable, once you have done what you can to make amends, to put the past behind you and continue with this positive lifestyle because you *want* to, and not solely because you are atoning for earlier misdeeds.

——— *Major cause of ill-health* ———

Even when we try to push it to the back of our minds, guilt is always with us, waiting to interfere with our enjoyment of life again, it is extremely damaging to all aspects of our health. As Dr Vernon Coleman says in his book *Mind Over Body*:

> Guilt is a major cause of heart disease, stomach ulceration, asthma, skin conditions and a hundred and one other problems.

The effect on our mental state can also be great. One woman who consulted me was so overwhelmed by feelings of inadequacy that she had become a workaholic who pushed herself harder and harder until she finally collapsed from exhaustion. She was then compelled to take time off work and rely on State benefit – which caused her to feel even more guilty. Had she been able to think more rationally about herself and her abilities, she would have realised that we all have different skills and talents, and that no one of us is worth more than any other person. Provided she committed herself to doing the best she could in her chosen field, she would have every reason to be proud of herself and the need for that self-induced excess of pressure would disappear.

Christine – perfectionist in a panic

Another patient of mine, whom I shall call Christine, was 40 years old when she first came to see me. She was suffering from an extreme anxiety state with frequent panic attacks, which were growing progressively worse.

Christine was a highly successful business consultant, intelligent, articulate, and always elegantly dressed and well made-up. Accustomed to thinking of herself as an achiever, she found her inability to control these panic attacks very difficult to cope with. In fact, her first words to me were, 'I feel so stupid.'

It emerged that Christine's father was a dour and authoritarian

2

man. A university lecturer always respected for his academic ability, he expected the same high standard of his only daughter. And Christine did turn out to be an excellent student who worked hard and was a high achiever in every subject. But the better she did, the more her father seemed to expect. Eventually it reached the stage where, running home from school excitedly to show her father the 97 per cent she had received for a piece of work, Christine was confronted with the scathing remark that, 'If you could get 97 per cent, you could have got 100 per cent.'

Perhaps her father really thought that this was the way to spur his daughter on to achieve even higher results; perhaps he was trying to keep her in her place – or perhaps he was a malicious man who delighted in making her feel small. Whatever the reason for his behaviour, he had created in his daughter a terror of anything less than perfection which lasted well into her adult life and was ultimately responsible for her anxiety state.

Amazingly, it had never occurred to Christine to question his reactions to her achievements. All young children tend to accept that what their parents do or say is correct but they normally begin to rebel against blind acceptance as they grow older. Christine never had. Possibly because of her awe – even fear – of her father, she merely assumed that he must be right and that she, therefore, must be wrong.

As we worked together she came to realise that, even if his motives had been the best, he had no right to belittle her genuine effort in the way that he had. Christine was at last able to put his views into perspective and to give herself credit for what she had achieved. Re-introducing this sense of self confidence and control into her life enabled her, over several weeks, to eliminate the panic attacks and bouts of anxiety.

—— *Are you troubled by guilt?* ——

Whether the guilt you experience is justified or whether it is the result of accidental or deliberate manipulation by someone else, until you stop and think about what makes you feel guilty, the effect on you is likely to continue.

Pause now and consider whether you are being troubled by feelings of guilt – without at this point analysing whether they are justified. Below are given some of the ways in which they might show themselves in your everyday life. You may:

- Find it difficult to make decisions.

- Feel that you are not fulfilling your potential.

- Always put other people before yourself.

- Worry too much about what *might* happen.

- Be easily influenced by others.

- Dwell on past mistakes.

- Lack confidence.

- Feel that you always let other people down.

- Be terrified of rejection.

- Be extremely sensitive to criticism.

- Wish that your skills were greater.

- Be far harder on yourself than on other people.

- Be easily intimated.

- Feel that you are less talented than anyone else you know.

If any or all of the above apply to you (on a regular basis as opposed to occasionally) then you are likely to be suffering from the effects of guilt. Whether that guilt is conscious or subconscious, self-induced or the outcome of someone else's attitude, the fact is that it exists and, until you do something about it, it will go on adversely affecting your life.

Fortunately, it *is* possible to do something about it, and I hope that, by reading this book and putting into practice those techniques which you feel apply to you, you will be able to come to terms with your own deeper emotions.

—— *Taking control of your life* ——

As you saw from Christine's story, the way you interact with other people can be coloured by the first real relationship you ever experienced – with your parents (or those who stood in that position). If they did all they could to show you that you were loved and appreciated (though they may have scolded you when you were naughty), you are likely to have a good self-image. Therefore you will be able to enjoy good relationships with others – not only in terms of one-to-one loving relationships but also those calling into play other interpersonal skills – with friends, workmates, colleagues, children, authority figures. . . and so on.

However, if like Christine, you were made to feel unworthy or unlovable, your self-esteem might well have plummeted to such a level that you are experiencing difficulty in one or more of the relationship areas indicated.

It is good to bear in mind therefore, that although you could not help being influenced by other people when you were very young, as an adult you can *choose* how much you allow this to happen. Such influence, whether it takes the form of emotional blackmail or constant criticism, is only effective if you allow it to be.

Suppose someone says to you 'What you did today was stupid.' Can that really do you harm? I think not, since you can choose to ignore it. What really hurts is your own thought process which usually follows such words. You think to yourself: Was I stupid? Did I make a complete fool of myself? I wonder if everyone else noticed. I wonder how they will think of me from now on. Eventually you may convince yourself that no one is ever going to think highly of you again – and all because of someone else's words.

—— *Various forms of criticism* ——

Criticism may be just or unjust, constructive or destructive, objective or judgmental. To prevent them from making you feel guilty unnecessarily, each of these needs to be handled in a different way.

- *If a criticism is just and valid*, the only straightforward way of dealing with it is to acknowledge it and state what you intend to do to either to put things right or see that it doesn't happen again. For example: *'You're late for the third time this week.'* 'Yes, I am. I won't let it happen again and I'll work ten minutes later today.'

- *A criticism which is unjust* is more difficult to handle because the natural tendency is to become heated in your own defence. Unfortunately, unless you happen to be an aggressive person to start with, the more heated you become, the more you are likely to lose control and say something foolish – which would then put you in the wrong. So remain calm, take a deep breath and do one of two things:

  1 If you are clear as to what your critic is complaining about, put your side of the story as quietly and succinctly as possible;

  2 If you do not understand the background to the criticism in the first place, ask for clarification; then you can go on to deal with it as above.

- *A constructive criticism,* although probably not pleasant to hear, is often made with good intentions and can be helpful in the long run. So resist your inclination to leap immediately to your own defence and give yourself time to think about what has been said. If you are at all upset, play for time by telling your critic that you will think about it and get back to him or her later.

- *A destructive criticism* is often an indication of the insecurity of the critic and can really be ignored. You can often recognise such criticisms because they tend to become a string of complaints punctuated with 'and' and 'but', and often growing more ridiculous in the process. Of course, if the critic is your boss, you may not be able to turn your back and walk away but at least, while you are obliged to listen, you can know deep in your inner self that there is nothing for you to reproach yourself with.

- *Criticisms which are basically objective* can become peppered with judgmental comments which no one has a right to make and which you can ignore – even if there is some basis of truth in the criticism itself. Returning to our earlier example, suppose your critic says: *'You've been late three times this week. You're always late. You're absolutely hopeless.'* The truth probably lies in the first sentence: *'You've been late three times this week.'* Telling you that you are always late is probably an exaggeration and saying that you are absolutely hopeless is a judgment which does not have to be taken into consideration. Assuming that you actually have been late three times in a single week, you can only respond to that part of the criticism as indicated earlier, by apologising, promising not to let it happen in the future and saying what you intend to do to make up for it.

It is easy to see, therefore, that whether or not we feel guilty is governed to a large extent by the words and attitudes of other people. But it is important to realise that none of them can do it alone. To make you feel guilty these people require your help so it is up to you to be aware of what is happening and not to give them that help. This doesn't mean that you may not regret something or want to make amends but it does mean that you will not waste your precious time and energy on fruitless guilt. You will have to be particularly on your guard against criticism that is repeated many times.

Repetitive criticism erodes confidence

If – either in your personal or business life – you are compelled to be in the company of someone who repeatedly finds fault with you, however much you try to shut your mind to their words, they will penetrate your subconscious until you may eventually find yourself accepting the statement as truth rather than as someone else's opinion. This applies even when, at the outset, you know perfectly well that they are being unreasonable. Repetition is highly effective. (That is why it is so often used in a positive way – as in affirmations, for example.)

One middle-aged woman I met told me that her husband had been telling her for the last 15 years that she was 'useless'. She was an intelligent woman, holding down a good job while running a home and bringing up three children. Hardly someone who could be considered useless. In the beginning she had ignored her husband's words, seeing them for what they were – an attempt to make himself feel superior. But, as time went on, the constant repetition of the criticism eroded her confidence until she really began to feel that she was useless.

Positive repetition pays dividends

The good news is that if negative repetition can be so effective, it follows that positive repetition must be equally so. So if you find yourself in a position where you are unable to escape the constant 'drip, drip' of negative accusations, you can take steps to counteract it so that it does you no harm.

Start by making a list of your good points – and don't be modest – we all have some. Write down the things you do well and the things you like about yourself. Then, whenever you have been the victim of someone else's unjustly critical words, choose any of those points and repeat it to yourself over and over again. It doesn't matter whether it is something specific: 'I'm a good friend', 'I can cook well', 'People enjoy my company'; or more general: 'I'm a nice person'. If you say it to yourself often enough, you will go a long way towards counteracting the other person's criticism. And you will certainly stop the really harmful result of such criticism – the negative words you would otherwise say to yourself when the other person has finished speaking.

Repeat positive affirmations, such as, 'I will succeed' or 'I am a terrific person' 20 times in succession and post written affirmations somewhere where you will see them often – the bathroom mirror or the fridge door.

When you go to bed at night, do you go over the day in your mind, and automatically focus on all the things which have gone wrong? You know the sort of thing: 'I wish I hadn't said. . .', 'I felt such a fool when. . .'. Stop! Make a definite commitment that from now on you will end your day on positive thoughts. Make a point of going over the things which have gone well for you during the day. They don't have to be great, earth-shaking happenings. They can be as minor as completing all the filing or weeding the flower-bed. Since we are incapable of thinking of more than one thing at a time, if you fill your mind with such positive thoughts, the negative ones will no longer be able to intrude.

Another good reason for indulging in this positive thinking process just before going to sleep is that, even when you are asleep and are no longer conscious of those thoughts, their positive and image-boosting effect will continue in your subconscious mind. In consequence, your sleep is likely to be deeper and more relaxed and you are more likely to wake as the confident person you have the right to be.

Guilt and Fear

Guilt doesn't stand alone. It is linked with many of the other emotions but predominantly that of fear. Both are destructive, both can cause actual physical problems, and both can result in a sad and stunted life rather than one which is positive and fulfilling. The fearful person is not anxious just in one area of life; the same anxiety tends to spill over into all aspects, so that she is afraid to make progress, accept change or fall in love. If this is how you have been feeling, do consider what Dr Susan Jeffers says in her book *Feel the Fear and Do It Anyway*: 'Pushing through fear is less frightening than living with the underlying fear that comes from a feeling of helplessness.'

Change is a part of life. We all change and develop as we grow older. Some changes are deliberate: such as deciding to live somewhere different, look for a new job, commit yourself to a new partner, have a baby. . .and so on. Others are involuntary, and may be good or bad: winning the pools or being made redundant, being offered a wonderful job, having an accident, inheriting a legacy or losing a loved one. There are also changes which are progressive and inevitable: we are all going to grow older – with the benefits and the problems that creates – and we are all going to die.

The fearful person cannot cope with change, seeing only the negative in any prospective situation while ignoring the positive. For example, a giant win on the pools may be a dream for many but all the fearful person can think of is the problems it may cause: will it alienate her from her friends, how will she cope with the begging letters, will people only want to know her for her money in future? Of course, these possibilities need to be considered, but with reasonable thought and proper advice, such situations can be handled quite successfully, leaving the winner to enjoy the positive aspects of such good fortune. But the fact that her mind is full of the possible problems not only makes it likely that she will make wrong decisions, it will take away any of the pleasure usually associated with the win.

Because fearful people are so resistant to change, they may well stay with what they know, even when the current state of affairs is disastrous. Many people find it hard to understand how a woman who is being beaten and abused by a tyrant of a husband or partner can remain in the situation for so long. But when the victim's self-esteem has been eroded over a long period, somehow her inner self comes to believe that this is how she deserves to be treated. And so, in many cases, she stays and allows the torment to continue. Thus we have the creation of a vicious circle – the longer she stays, the more her self-esteem disintegrates and the less able she is to do anything to change her circumstances.

Fear has nothing to do with logic, which it systematically destroys, but it influences every decision the sufferer makes. She will know at one level that she is not being logical and that she is allowing her fear to govern her life. But this simply increases her sense of inadequacy and powerlessness, and her self-image deteriorates still further.

Josie's story – phobic reactions

Josie was just such a sufferer. An only child, she had a father who always seemed to be at work, arriving home each day after his daughter was in bed and often working at weekends. Her mother was an undemonstrative woman who would punish Josie for any misdemeanour by refusing to speak to her at all – and this silent treatment could last for days. When telling me about her upbringing, Josie still became tearful even though she was now in her late thirties.

Because her mother would not speak to her at all, the child sometimes did not even know why she was being punished. And, once the silence was broken and things were back to normal, she did not dare ask her mother what she had done wrong, in case the whole sequence of events started again.

Naturally, Josie never felt able to invite friends to her home, because she never knew whether her mother would be speaking or not. Eventually the other children stopped inviting her and she became more and more isolated. In her teens the periods of silence became ever more frequent and Josie became even more isolated and more introverted. Feeling herself rejected on all sides, her self-esteem plummeted and she considered herself unworthy and inadequate.

Josie began to be afraid of going out in case the people she encountered also rejected her. When necessity caused her to venture out, she was so fearful of things going wrong that she became tense and anxious – and so, of course, they *did* go wrong. Only minor things perhaps, like forgetting what she wanted or dropping her purchases in a busy shop, but enough to make her feel even more inferior.

She began to dread going out so much that her subconscious mind began to invent reasons to prevent her doing so, until it reached the point where Josie was a virtual prisoner in her own silent home.

I realise that Josie's is quite an extreme example but there are many people whose background causes them to be so afraid of life that they develop more and more fears as time goes by.

Overcoming Fear

If excessive fear has its foundation in childhood, the original cause may well have been long forgotten but the effect continues until something deliberate is done to overcome it. The sufferer will misdirect that fear and apply it to present situations when really it belongs solely to the past. It will tend to affect every area of life, as it did in Josie's case. Such accumulated fear can be overcome with the aid of counselling, hypnotherapy or psychotherapy if the sufferer will seek such help – as Josie eventually did. The stumbling block usually arises when their inherent negativity leads them to believe that they are past such assistance and that no one and nothing can help them.

Fear such as this can lead to a variety of problems. Some people may suffer from excess stress with all its associated aches and pains. Some may become insomniacs. Others suffer anxiety and panic attacks. In extreme cases panic can cause the sufferer to hyperventilate and to feel that they are going to pass out – indeed, they well might.

Because of all the problems fear and guilt bring in their wake, you can readily realise why it is essential to deal with them before they take control of your life. Read on! Help is at hand.

— 2 —

Growing Up
with Guilt

The law of every civilised country states that a person is innocent until proved guilty, yet still there are many individuals who burden themselves with feelings of guilt whether or not those feelings are justified. Most of the guilt of the present is based upon opinions of the past. In the majority of cases those opinions were someone else's. Current guilt is a form of self-punishment which is continuing a process started long ago, usually in childhood.

—— *Sowing seeds of self-doubt* ——

The seeds of our adult self-image are usually sown very early, and it is not difficult to see why. As a child you naturally believed that all grown-ups were so wise that they must have known what they were talking about. Even when, as an adult, you come to realise that even the best-intentioned of us can be mistaken, there is still within you a child listening to those long-ago words.

As a child you had no choice but to conform and do what you were told. In the majority of cases this is just as it should be – how else can a child be taught what is wrong and what is right, how to behave and how to remain safe? But there are cases, of course, where what the child is told to do is wrong. Sometimes she is able to sense this but is powerless to do anything about it; at others she will be so accustomed to doing what others bid her that she will not even question their instructions.

In Chapter One we looked at the case of Christine and the way in which she reacted to her autocratic father. But not everyone reacts in the same way to the same basic set of circumstances, as you will see from the case which follows.

Wendy – Conditioned to contempt

Wendy's father was always telling her how stupid she was. A girl of reasonable intelligence, she started by doing quite well at her primary school. But as the months and years went by, her confidence was eroded by her father's thoughtless words; the more she tried, the more he belittled her efforts. The result was that Wendy grew up to be someone who had no belief in herself and her abilities.

Unfortunately, as often happens in such cases, Wendy eventually co-habited with a man who continued the treatment begun by her father all those years ago. This is hardly surprising, as her inner feelings about herself were that she really was stupid and inadequate. It didn't matter that she had passed her exams at school. It didn't matter that she had obtained and held down a good job. It didn't matter that her boss had told her that she was doing so well that she was being considered for promotion. All these things were accepted by her logical mind but could not overcome her innermost thoughts. In fact, she began to believe herself to be a fraud, fooling the people around her, and she lived in a state of perpetual stress, waiting to be found out as the 'stupid person' she really was.

Had Wendy met a man who thought she was wonderful and who said so and treated her as though this was the case, she would not have been able to cope with such a novel situation. She would have had no respect for someone whose opinion did not accord with those inner feelings which resulted from her father's early words. It was only when she became involved with a man who treated her with contempt and disdain that she felt inwardly comfortable – even though her outer self was hurt and dismayed by his words and attitude.

We saw in Chapter One, that change is usually uncomfortable and often difficult, and so Wendy continued to put up with the way her boyfriend treated her rather than face the situation and make some changes to her self-image. It was only after she consulted her doctor in the hope that he would give her something to calm her nerves that, on his recommendation, she came to see me.

Therapy: Getting things into proportion

I have said that change is difficult and uncomfortable. But you can change if you really need to, and want to – and are prepared to work at it. And, once the change has been made, your life will probably be far happier.

In Wendy's case, I took her back by means of hypnosis to look again at her childhood. (This does not have to be as traumatic or painful as it sounds, because it is possible to ensure that the patient 'sees' it all as an observer and does not have to 're-live' any distress or humiliation she may have felt at the time.) Once we had reached the point, we used the following method to minimise the damaging effect of her boorish father and his words.

- I asked Wendy to view the picture of herself and her father as if it were on a cinema or television screen and to describe it to me. She naturally spoke of the 'little girl' and the 'big man', and this was how it had seemed to her at the time. The little girl, of course, would never have dared to answer back to the big man, whatever he said to her.

- Next, I asked her to continue watching the picture but gradually to make the big man diminish in stature while the little girl grew bigger and bigger, until the two were of similar size. I suggested to her that, being equal in size, she was now able to respond in any way she wished to the man and – speaking aloud – she told him that he was wrong and that she was not stupid at all. He was to leave her alone and not say such things any more.

- Following that, I suggested to Wendy that she should make the little girl larger in size than the man. What would she like to say now? She told me that she could not be bothered to speak to him at all. She felt pity for him because the only way he could make himself feel big was to be horrible to her, but he seemed so pathetic that what he said had no effect.

Even this first attempt at putting the past in its proper perspective made Wendy feel a great deal better. But, if you wish to change the pattern imprinted on your subconscious, the process has to be repeated several times. I have usually found, when working with patients, that if the same positive information is fed into the subconscious daily for a period of about three weeks, it is sufficient to eradicate the harmful effects of the images previously prevailing.

As Wendy's confidence grew, she began to re-think many areas of her life – particularly where relationships were concerned. She decided that she was not prepared to continue being treated so badly by her boyfriend and issued an ultimatum that he either change or go. He didn't change – and so he went!

— *Self-help: questions and answers* —

It is very clear then, that even if the person who instilled those original feelings of guilt is no longer around, we may still allow that person to have an effect upon us. And doing so increases our vulnerability to the moods of all other people so that, should they become angry, we automatically react as though they must be right without stopping to consider the realities of the situation.

If you feel that you have a tendency to react to others in this way, ask yourself the following questions:

- *Am I excessively sensitive to criticism?* None of us enjoys being criticised, and the instinctive reaction is often to argue or rebel against it. But we also know that sometimes we are in the wrong, and that justified and constructive criticism can be helpful. However, if you find yourself automatically believing every criticism levelled at you without questioning it, it could be that you are reacting to voices from the past as well as from the present.

- *Do I feel that everyone else knows better than I do?* Here again, there is a difference between having due respect for someone who is an expert in a particular field and believing that everyone is wiser and cleverer than you are.

- *Looking back over my life, was there one person (or more than one) who repeatedly made me feel inferior?* You may have to do this in stages, for often the originator of the downward spiral has been 'forgotten' or pushed to the back of your mind. Go back to the last person who made you feel this way and then see if that was an echo of someone prior to that. Continue in this way as far back as you can go – although, if you have no conscious memory of your early childhood, it may be necessary to seek professional help to reach the earliest causes.

- *I understand that, because I was small and powerless at the time, that person's will always prevailed over mine. Do I really want this pattern to continue?* Although it is not possible to alter what happened in the past – it *is* possible to alter your inner perception of it. At that time you almost certainly had no choice about the way in which you reacted. You have that choice now.

- *Am I prepared to work to change my inner view of myself?* As we have seen, it does take effort on your part. But it is possible to change and more quickly than you might have believed. If your answer to this question is 'yes', you will find specific self-help techniques detailed at the end of this chapter.

Once you have discovered the original cause of your guilt feelings, you will have increased your knowledge of yourself and your awareness. You may well also be asking yourself why all this should have happened to you – why you should be the one who was made to feel inferior and lacking in confidence. I wonder what answers you come up with.

Whatever your personal conclusions may be, remember that it is by overcoming the problems we encounter in life that we are able to grow and develop, in a practical or spiritual sense, or perhaps both at the same time.

—— *Daring to take calculated risks* ——

In a practical sense, overcoming self-image problems makes you stronger and able to deal more effectively with the slings and arrows of life. It also helps you to change the direction of your life at will rather than be tossed about on a sea of chance. As opportunities arise, you will be more inclined to grasp them. Indeed, if no opportunities present themselves, you will be confident enough to go out there and create them.

You will become assertive enough to take calculated risks, knowing that you will not always succeed but enjoying the prospect and the actuality of trying, revelling in the successes and learning from the failures.

Having been through all the problems yourself, you will become a far nicer person and be more able to empathise with others and their difficulties. Whether you wish to develop this skill so that you set about helping others in a deliberate way or simply to ensure that those you care about do not suffer in the way you suffered, this has to be a positive and beneficial attitude.

Sylvia, for example, has worked hard to overcome the effects of always being unfavourably compared to her older brother. Now that she has children of her own, she told me of the deliberate efforts she is making to help each of them develop a strong and positive self-image.

Although she knows herself to be a good and loving mother, Sylvia realised that she had fallen into the trap of commenting far more on their negative aspects than the positive ones. It is something many of us do. How often do we say to our children, 'Your room is in a terrible mess', 'Why haven't you done your homework yet?', 'You can't go out looking like that'? I am not suggesting that these things do not need saying but why don't we also remember to say, 'Thank you for tidying you room', 'Finished your homework? Well done!' or 'You look nice today'? The majority of us rarely think of praising, except for major achievements. If our children love us and take heed of our words, what are we doing to their self-image?

One of the ways in which Sylvia decided to change, was to make a conscious effort to find something positive to say to each child every day. She also made a point of displaying all the paintings, collages or handicrafts they brought home from school or playgroup. And, most important of all, she told them frequently that she loved them.

Spiritual benefits

What you consider to be the spiritual benefits of self-knowledge, will depend on your personal beliefs. I am not using the word 'spiritual' here in the context of any particular religion but more as an awareness which guides us on our journey through this life – and whatever may come after it. Of course, you may believe that when you die all is ended – and you have every right to such a belief. Most people, however, have a feeling that there is something more to come, even if they are slightly confused about what it will be.

Let's assume for the moment that your current life is simply one step on a giant pathway to eternity. If that is the case, then there are bound to be some parts of that pathway which are easy to travel while others present obstacles that have to be overcome. But, just because some parts of the path are more difficult or tire you, that doesn't mean that you cannot persist in your journey along it and eventually reach your destination.

If you believe that we all have more than a single life try thinking of each individual one as a class at school. Only when we have learned the lessons taught in class one are we ready to go on to class two. . . and so on, until we reach the top of the school. Perhaps the lesson of this 'class' is how to deal with and overcome a sense of guilt.

Even if you cannot accept the concept of several incarnations, look on this stage in your life as part of a similar learning process. Until you have conquered this particular part of your personal curriculum you will not be ready to progress to the next one.

Whatever your spiritual beliefs, remember that although something may seem exceedingly difficult to us at the time, when we look back on it later we wonder what all the fuss was about. To the pupil taking GCSE examinations, it seems that nothing could be more wearing and more difficult. But three or four years later, when that same student may be at college or university, she will look back and realise that what she fretted over so long ago was simple compared to what she is required to do now.

And so it will be with you. If you suffer now from the effects of guilt – however it was caused – overcoming those effects may seem an enormous undertaking. But, provided you persevere and complete the task, I promise you that the time will come when all these negative feelings will be no more than distant memories.

Childhood abuse

A problem which has come increasingly to the fore over the last few years is that of childhood abuse. This does not necessarily mean that abuse is on the increase; it could be simply that people are more willing to talk about it. In the past, victims and their families were so concerned with the 'shame' of the situation that they tried to conceal it and act as if nothing had happened. This, of course, made the situation even worse for the unfortunate victims of the abuse, as it convinced them of what they already felt

– that they should feel guilty and ashamed because of what had been done to them.

Any child who is the victim of abuse – particularly sexual abuse – experiences many emotions (see also Chapter Eight). And one of the most predominant is guilt. Even though, in later life, the child may realise that the fault was not hers but that of the perpetrator, her subconscious mind will still be filled with guilt. After all, the offence was committed by a grown-up and the child is convinced that grown-ups know everything and are always in the right. If one of these all-knowing people – particularly if a close relative – has abused the child, she will inwardly believe that she deserved that abuse. Such a feeling is often reinforced by the abuser, who will caution the child not to talk to anyone else about what has happened. He will say that people will not believe her and that, even if they do, she will be considered a 'bad person'. Such words, naturally, reinforce the already present sense of guilt the child is experiencing.

The one thing an abused child does not feel is anger. If told that it is 'her fault' or that she is 'bad', she will accept this and will go on accepting it inwardly throughout the coming years, whatever logic and experience tell her.

In her book *Positive Thinking*, Vera Peiffer states: 'Just because your parents are your parents does not mean that they can abuse you and still expect to be loved.' Indeed, the one way in which the adult who was an abused child can learn to undo much of the damage is by experiencing anger against the person who was the perpetrator of the abuse. This does not cause her to forget the past – in fact it would not be healthy to block it completely from her mind – but it does help her to come to terms with it, then put it aside and prevent it affecting the remainder of her life.

The person at whom she learns to feel angry does not even have to be present. It does not matter whether they are still on the scene at all – or even if they are dead. The process is still effective, and is another of the techniques which will be explained at the end of this chapter.

Not a nice girl

Charlotte's situation was slightly different from those I usually encounter among my patients. A smartly-dressed, intelligent woman of 32, she originally came to consult me about the problems she had with relationships. She told me that she seemed to enter one disastrous relationship after another and, even though she was aware that the men were not right for her, she seemed powerless to do anything about it.

The three men with whom Charlotte had had long-term relationships were all abusers in their own way. One had a problem with alcohol and when drunk would become physically violent. The second had a terrible temper and would swear at Charlotte and do his best to humiliate her. The third had actually raped her on two occasions during the course of their engagement.

You might wonder why an otherwise intelligent woman allowed herself to be treated in such a way. Indeed, Charlotte herself could not understand her tendency to be attracted to men who logic told her would cause her pain and trouble. During the course of her therapy, however, the underlying cause became obvious.

Charlotte had a cousin Simon who was some five years older than she was, and as children they both used to spend part of the summer holiday at their grandmother's house by the sea. One year, when Charlotte was eight and Simon 13, she had been taking a shower when her cousin came into the bathroom. This had not worried her as, having been practically brought up together, they had often seen each other naked and thought nothing of it.

However, on this occasion Simon had wanted to touch her and stroke her. A naturally affectionate little girl and fond of her cousin, Charlotte had not found anything wrong in this.

During that holiday, whenever they were alone together, Simon had taken the opportunity to hold, kiss and caress his younger cousin. On the one occasion when he had tried to take things even further, Charlotte had protested and the boy immediately stopped.

The eight-year-old girl had not seen anything wrong in what had happened between her and the cousin she adored, and nothing was ever said to anyone else about it. It was only as Charlotte grew older and realised that Simon should not have acted as he did that she began to feel guilty. But her guilt was not so much for what had happened, but rather because she had actually enjoyed it. Logic told her that 'nice' girls did not behave in such a way, and, more particularly, that 'nice' girls never, ever enjoyed such things when they did happen.

Charlotte therefore became convinced in her inner mind that she was not and could never be a 'nice' girl. Once her subconscious was programmed to think in this way, she sought out men who would continue this programming – men who would not treat her as 'nice' girls deserved to be treated, men who would treat her badly.

During her counselling sessions I convinced Charlotte that, in fact, she had done nothing wrong. Most little girls like to be kissed and cuddled, particularly by people of whom they are already fond. Because Simon had never actually hurt her and had stopped at once when they reached a stage Charlotte did not want, she did not see him as a threat and merely responded as any affectionate child would.

Once Charlotte was able to understand that she did not have anything to feel guilty about, we worked on altering the self-image she had created over the years. This increased her self-esteem and confidence, and taught her to think of herself as someone who deserved to be treated with warmth and respect. Anyone who did not do so, had no place in her life.

—— *Dealing with past situations* ——

When a child has been made to feel guilty because of abuse by an adult – whether this was physical, emotional or sexual abuse – she (or he) experiences a lack of power and an inability to do anything about the situation. This sense of being powerless is likely to remain with her throughout her adult years and can be extremely limiting. It can cause her to see herself as – and therefore to become – a permanent loser in life.

The 'loser' will finally convince herself that it is wrong to have fun or to get any pleasure out of life. She will become extremely vulnerable to the moods of other people – if someone is angry with her, she will feel guilty without stopping to consider whether the anger is justified or not. She may be almost relieved to find that she has problems as this is what her inner mind tells her she deserves.

If you find yourself in this situation, what needs to be done is to look at the time when you were a child, but to see the past through the eyes of the adult you are now. Trying to shut the whole thing out of your mind may bring temporary relief but the problem will remain. As promised earlier, here are three techniques for dealing with such past situations. (I am assuming that you will by now have thought about the people and events of your past sufficiently to have worked out how the problems all began).

Starting point: learn to relax

The first stage in any of these self-help techniques is to learn to relax. Guilt brings great tension and unless it is released you will not be able to access your subconscious mind, which is where your self-image is lodged.

You may choose to go to a class in relaxation or use one of the many relaxation cassettes now on the market. If you prefer to work alone to achieve a relaxed state, the basic requirements are these.

1 Select a place and time where you are unlikely to be disturbed. If you wish it, you may have some gentle background music. Sit in a comfortable chair or lie on a bed and close your eyes.

2 It is far easier to relax a muscle which has first of all been tensed. So, starting with our feet and working upwards, tense

and relax each set of muscles in turn. Pay particular attention to those around your neck, shoulders, jaw and face as this is where tension is most often experienced. Take your time.

3 Now spend several moments concentrating on the rhythm of your breathing and ensuring that you breathe from your diaphragm rather than – as many of us do – from your upper chest. Become truly aware of your breathing, noting how your diaphragm rises as you breathe in, and falls as you breathe out.

You may need to practise relaxing for a few days before beginning to use one of the self-help techniques detailed below. But this is not time wasted, as the more you are able to relax, the easier it will be to reach the depths of your subconscious mind where all the negative programming exists. Only when you are able to relax at will should you progress to one of the techniques which follow.

Method 1

This is the one described earlier in this chapter, when I briefly detailed Wendy's therapy.

1 Create a 'photograph' in your mind of the situation which occurred when you were a child. See everything in as much detail as possible: yourself as you looked then, the person who caused you to lose your self-esteem, the room you were in.

Spend as much time as you need filling in the picture. Initially, if we are looking at an episode from your childhood, the other person is likely to be considerably larger than you.

2 Now make an adjustment so that you are bigger than you were while the other person, even though possibly still larger than you are, shrinks in size. Ask yourself how you feel about them now and whether they still seem so intimidating.

3 The next adjustment should be to make the two of you the same size so that you can confront each other as equals. Do

those words or actions still have the same devastating effect upon you when they emanate from someone no bigger than yourself?

4 Finally, adjust the picture still further so that you are now considerably larger than the other person. Remember the words spoken or the actions taken. What sort of effect do they now have coming as they do from such a small individual? Can they really bother you? Do you even have to listen to them?

Method 2

1 This time I would like you to create in your imagination a moving picture – as though you were watching a film or video. Once again, view everything in as much detail as possible – hearing the words, seeing the actions and remembering the way you felt. As we have already seen, the one emotion you probably did not feel at the time was anger; it is very difficult for a small child in a vulnerable position to experience anger at an adult.

2 Freeze the 'film' at what you consider to be the most crucial point – the point at which, had you been an adult, too, you would have become angry. Although the child on the screen is unable to become angry, the adult you are today can do so on that child's behalf. So put your current self into the picture too; face the aggressor and say everything you feel you want to say on behalf of the child. You might choose to speak the words aloud or you might prefer to imagine them as you look at the screen in your mind.

Method 3

1 Create in your imagination a large, coloured picture of the person you consider to have been the cause of your early loss of confidence. Look at the picture in your mind and ask yourself how you react and how that person makes you feel.

2 Now, still in your imagination, play the childhood game of drawing on a photograph. Add glasses, a beard, black gaps in the teeth, a Groucho Marx moustache – anything you like to make the figure ridiculous. Look at it once again and consider how you feel. Can someone who looks so ridiculous really cause you any distress? I doubt it.

You are not alone

One thing which those who have been victims of aggression or abuse in their early life often fail to realise is that they are not alone. Because it seemed disloyal – particularly when parents are involved – to talk to anyone about what happened in your childhood, you may have kept it all to yourself. But I can assure you that you are by no means alone. Ask any counsellor or therapist and they will tell you of countless cases where someone has had a sense of guilt or failure instilled in them because of the words or deeds of another person in their early years.

By pointing this out, I am not trying to minimise what you feel or the pain you may have experienced. But it often helps to realise that others have been victims in the same way that you have. Indeed, the flourishing of self-help groups would indicate that many people find comfort in talking about their problems. Perhaps you would, too. However, if you would find this awkward, you might consider talking to a good friend or seeking the aid of a professional counsellor.

As Dr Susan Jeffers says, in her book *Feel the Fear and Do It Anyway*: '. . . join the crowd! Fear seems to be epidemic in our society.' You are not alone. You are not 'different'. You are not 'bad'. You have been made to feel that way by the thoughtlessness or the deliberate unkindness of someone else. But, however much this may have affected you in the past, you should be proud that you have chosen not to let it affect you in the future.

— 3 —

Why Women
Carry More Guilt

I said in the Introduction that this sense of guilt exists far more among women than among men, and after 15 years of seeing patients for a wide variety of problems, I can assure you that it is a fact.

—— *So many difficult situations* ——

Perhaps, in generations still to come, all this will change (I doubt it – though the reasons for the sense of guilt may be different). But those of us who are women now will have been born into a world where the female role has changed extremely rapidly. Even young women will still have memories of mothers, aunts or grandmothers whose entire life was given over to looking after the home and raising the family. It is not so many years since divorce was almost unheard of and pregnancies either happened or they didn't – they were neither planned, prevented nor aborted. All this naturally played a great part in governing how a woman could live her life and, however much times have changed, those memories still have an effect upon women today.

Everyone has difficult decisions to make in life but women tend to have all the ones that men do – and plenty more of their own. In this chapter, let's look at just a few of them and some case histories of women who have faced such guilt.

—— *Teens and peer group pressures* ——

The teenage girl may be uncertain whether or not she should indulge in sex with her boyfriend. It has always been the case that more young people *say* they have done so than actually have – and this has always had an effect on both boys and girls. But it is girls who run the risk of pregnancy, when they are little more than children themselves. The media today is full of stories of teenage mothers. And when this undeniable evidence of sexual activity is combined with peer pressure, can the girl who holds back be blamed for wondering if she is 'different' or if there is something wrong with her? And the one thing no teenager likes to be is different from her peer group.

Think how inferior this must make the young girl who has never even had a date, let alone a sexual encounter. She won't stop to question whether her friends are telling the truth or not; she will hear the boasting, know that she has no such experiences to talk about – and feel different. I recently heard the mother of a *nine-year-old* girl telling a friend that her daughter was unhappy because she was the only one in her class without a boyfriend. At nine years of age! (See also Chapter Six)

Drugs

It is often peer pressure too which leads otherwise sensible youngsters to experiment with dangerous substances such as solvents or drugs. I once had to work with a thirteen-year-old girl who was in hospital recovering from a glue-sniffing incident. When asked by her tearful mother why she had been so foolish,

the girl said that for ages she had refused but had been so taunt-
ed and teased by others in her class at school that her life had
been made a misery. Eventually, she had given in to stop them
harassing her.

Shoplifting

Another case involved repeated incidences of shoplifting. Rachel
was a shy child and when she started at the local comprehensive
school she found it rather difficult to make friends. She would eye
from a distance people who seemed to fit in and mix easily with
others, and one group of girls in particular seemed to Rachel to
be all that she was not. They were always together and seemed to
be having a great deal of noisy fun.

When one of these girls asked if she would like to join their
'gang', Rachel was flattered and delighted. Then it transpired
that, to become a member, she would have to go into town with
them on Saturday and steal an item from one of the shops they
visited.

Rachel had been brought up to be honest and had never stolen
anything in her life. She did not want to start now, but she longed
to be part of what she saw as a wonderful group of potential
friends. So she gave in and did manage to steal a lipstick (something she never used) from a local store without being caught. But
this only made her feel worse as, knowing she had done something wrong, her guilt began to grow. She also discovered that the
gang went shoplifting every weekend and, although she no longer
wished to join them, they threatened to disclose what she had
done if she did not.

Smoking and drinking

If you want further evidence of how greatly we can be influenced
by other people, particularly when young, ask yourself why any
young girl ever begins to smoke. Very few actually enjoy the taste
of their first cigarettes. Also, it is an expensive hobby; and anyone able to read is now aware of the potential dangers which can

result from smoking. Yet they still do it. They do it in order to be like everyone else.

The same applies to heavy drinking. There is nothing wrong with alcohol in moderation if that is what you enjoy. But how many young girls going out with the crowd – or with a boy – would have the courage to say that they would prefer an alcohol-free drink? Very few.

——— *Career girl or home maker* ———

It is widely accepted now, that it is every woman's right to pursue a career of her own. She also has the right, of course, to choose a less demanding job – or, indeed, not to go out to work at all in order to devote most of her time to running a home. Why then, whichever choice she makes, is there usually someone who seems intent on making her feel that she has been selfish, thus inducing in her a sense of guilt? It may be the fault of an individual or of an element of the media but it often appears to the woman concerned that she just cannot win. If she decides to progress up the career ladder, she may be accused of being 'unfeminine' or of thinking only of herself. Yet, if she rejects this path to become predominantly a homemaker, she is told that she is wasting her education or not fulfilling her potential.

High-flier Janette

Janette faced just this problem. She did very well at university and was offered an excellent position in the research department of a pharmaceutical company. The salary was high and the prospects good. Janette herself was delighted. Until, that is, everyone else started voicing an opinion. Her parents, although proud of her achievements, had hoped that their daughter would settle down with Brian, her boyfriend, and give them grandchildren. They did not see the point in her becoming what her father called a 'high-flier'.

Brian himself indulged in emotional blackmail and tried to make Janette feel guilty for (as he put it) loving her job more than she loved him. Every magazine she opened seemed to contain homemaking hints and pictures of happy young mothers. The woman next door, whose husband had sadly been made redundant, even accused her of stealing a man's job.

It took all Janette's strength of character to stick to her belief in herself and her goals, and to overcome the guilt everyone else seemed ready to heap upon her. A less confident person might not have managed it and could have ended up doing a job she did not find fulfilling and eventually resenting those who had persuaded her to do so.

Stay-at-home wife and mother, Marian

Marian had never wanted anything other than to be a wife and mother. She was overjoyed when she gave birth to twin boys, and decided not to return to her job but to look after them full-time. Her husband, John, was happy for her to do whatever she wished, and they were fortunate that his income was sufficient for her to be able to make the choice.

Other people, however, had different ideas. Her former boss seemed to take it as a personal insult that Marian was not returning to work, although he had no trouble in finding her replacement. Friends were amazed when, having asked her when she was going back to work, she informed them that she intended to be a full-time mother. They acted as though she were letting them down in some way.

—— *Be mistress of your own fate* ——

Why should a woman be criticised for following her own instincts, whether to be a career woman, a wife and mother or to combine the two? And yet it happens. The Marians of this world are made to feel small on many occasions. When you meet somebody new, what is one of the first things they are likely to ask? 'What do you do?' Very few women have the confidence to state proudly, 'I'm a mother.' Most murmur apologetically, 'Oh, I'm just a housewife.'

If a housewife is what you choose to be, and if you do it to the best of your ability, then be proud of the fact. If you would rather pursue a fulfilling career and pay someone else to do the housework or to look after your children, then you have every right to be proud of that, too. The most important thing is to be honest with yourself and, having made your decision, not to allow *anyone* – friend, relative, boss or journalist – to make you feel that you are the odd one out or have done something wrong.

—— *Superwoman and New Man* ——

What about the women who try to combine the two – home and career? Why should they be made to feel guilty if they buy ready-prepared food instead of spending hours in the kitchen after a day at work? Like the teenage girl who thinks that everyone else is having brilliant sex, the working homemaker tends to feel that while she struggles to maintain both roles every other woman manages to achieve excellence in both areas.

Television commercials do not help her sagging spirits. They depict a beautiful and beautifully tailored and made-up career woman arriving home at the end of the day still in top form, dancing through a gleamingly immaculate house while throwing off her designer suit. She showers, revealing a perfect body, then steps into another designer outfit. She then passes lightly into the spotless kitchen to create a home-cooked three course meal for herself, the gorgeous man in her life and three or four beautiful friends – or she is taken out on the town. Is it any wonder many women feel inadequate?

It doesn't even matter that their logical brains tell them that real life is not like this and that many of their sisters put on their slippers and sit with a tray on their lap eating something which took no more than ten minutes to prepare. Just as the power of criticism lies in its repetition, the more times one sees such a commercial the greater its effect is likely to be – particularly if there is already an underlying sense of failure. After all, if repeating television commercials was not considered to be effective, why would so many companies spend hundreds of thousands of pounds doing just that?

And we all know that New Man is supposed to share the home chores equally with the woman but survey after survey reveals that this is not what actually happens. Of course, there are some men who do pull their weight, just as there are some who choose to take on the greater proportion of household work or child care, but such men are certainly in the minority.

—— *Children: to have or have not* ——

Many years ago, before the pill, advanced fertility treatment and legal abortions, there was far less of a decision to be made about when (and, indeed, whether) to have children. I am not saying that this state of affairs was not the cause of many a heartache; it was. However, it did induce less stress in women in terms of possible sense of guilt about the decisions they made; the options were far fewer.

For some women there is no problem, even today. They know just what they want to do about having children. But for many there are any number of decisions to be made:

• *Do I want children at all?* If I decide that I do not, am I being 'unnatural'? (Someone is bound to tell her that she is.) Will I regret that decision when I am older and it is too late?

- *If I do want children, when do I want to have them?* While I am still young enough to be really active with them? (But then will I miss out on a career?) Should I wait until I am older when it might possibly be more difficult to conceive? Will I want to abandon my career after progressing in it? If I have a child at 40, I will probably be a pensioner before it leaves home. And how will the child react when it realises that mother is a lot older than the other mothers? How will I feel about that myself?

- *If I decide to have children, should I return to work,* and at what point? Do I really want someone else to look after my babies? Will I miss out on opportunities if I don't continue working as soon as possible? Will I become boring to be with, if my entire life is made up of home and family? How will I feel if I miss their first words and first steps?

Annie and the nanny

Annie and Martin both had good jobs which they enjoyed. Annie had returned to work a few weeks after the birth of each of their two little girls, leaving a nanny to take care of the children. The arrangement seemed to work very well. The children were well cared for, healthy and happy. Annie and Martin progressed up their respective corporate ladders. Then, one Sunday afternoon when they were all in the garden, three-year-old Natasha fell and grazed her knees. Annie instinctively bent down and opened her arms to her daughter – but the child rushed to seek comfort in the arms of the nanny.

Although Annie was pleased that the nanny-child relationship was so warm and caring, she was hurt and surprised that little Natasha had completely ignored *her* when she needed comfort. She told me later, 'I felt a physical pain which would not go away.' Although she and Martin had been doing their very best for their children, Annie felt guilty.

Not all women suffer angst in such situations – but they are in the minority. For the majority there is no perfect answer, so all

36

they can do is whatever seems best at the time. That is often hard enough in itself but it can be made many times worse by the effect of the words of other people – however well-meaning.

—— *Positive and negative energy* ——

Perhaps it is a side-effect of wanting to be all things to all people that causes so many women to feel that they have to be doing something useful all the time. You know the type of thing: 'I can't sit and watch television unless I am doing the mending or knitting a sweater'; 'If I stay in bed for an extra 20 minutes, I use the time to write the weekly shopping list'.

There are many rules in life to which you may choose to adhere, be they the commandments given in the Bible or the rules of civilised society. But I have yet to hear of the one which says: 'Thou shalt not have an extra hour in bed on Sunday morning'. I am not advocating that you turn into a complete slob but a little self-indulgence does no harm – and can often make you feel extremely good – provided, of course, you do not feel guilty about it. And why should you?

Each of us has a certain amount of emotional energy to expend during the course of the day. Positive use of that energy creates a sense of well-being which brings about an even greater supply. Negative use, however, depletes our existing store. That is why, if you have experienced extreme anger or suffered a fit of sadness, you feel drained and exhausted, whereas a happy experience can make you feel mentally bright and alert, even though you may be physically tired.

A sense of guilt is one of the most destructive uses of energy. In itself it achieves nothing but, because it tends to be an on-going condition as opposed to a fleeting one, it can cause you to feel permanently exhausted. The life-energy you have is a very precious gift; don't fritter it away on such a non-constructive and draining emotion as guilt.

—— *Solving personal problems* ——

Life is full of decisions and many of them can be quite difficult to make. Those which involve only you may seem on the surface to be easier but are they? It is when you are faced with a decision which affects you and no one else that you have to take full responsibility. You may listen to what other people have to say – although this often causes even more confusion – but in the end you have to make up your own mind.

What is the best way to go about solving those problems which are predominantly yours alone? Problems such as those we have already looked at, and others such as whether to change your job, return to studying or put an elderly relative into a residential home. Some of these decisions do concern other people to a greater or lesser degree but, in many cases, their final solution is up to you. And it is for that very reason that, having made them, you are often left feeling selfish – and guilty.

To find the best solution at the time, you need to ask yourself a series of questions – and to give yourself absolutely honest answers. To show you how the same questions (see next page) work for different situations, let us apply them to two of the problem areas already mentioned and two different women:

Alison was married to Tim and they had two young sons, aged six and eight. Before the children were born, Alison worked in a local bank where she had been promoted twice. She took time off to have her children and stayed at home with them until the younger one was at primary school. Now she was ready to return to work, and everyone – from her husband and her mother to her former employer – was anxious for her to continue climbing the rungs of the banking ladder. Alison was not sure what she wanted. Should she 'fulfil her potential' or should she settle for a lesser job which would allow her more time with her sons?

Vivienne, recently divorced, felt that she was at a crossroads. She had worked as a schoolteacher since leaving college but, now that her son and daughter were young adults living away from home, she had the urge to do something more adventurous with her life. She had a great longing to travel and was considering letting her flat and just 'taking off' to see as much of the world as she could before her savings ran out. Everyone else told her that she was mad even to contemplate such a thing and she had heard it so often that she almost began to believe it herself.

Questions and answers

- *If no one else was involved in any way, what would I really like to do?*
  Alison first said that what she really wanted was to get the kind of job which would allow her to be home before her sons returned from school and give her extra time off during the school holidays. She felt that probably part-time or temporary work would be the answer. But, after thinking a little more, she told me that she did not really want to go back to work at all. This was not laziness but a desire to be a full-time wife and mother - possibly taking on some voluntary work as well.

  Vivienne had no doubts whatsoever. She wanted to see far-off distant places such as China, India and Australia.

- *Who else is involved and in what way?*
  Alison came up with a great, long list of people. Tim: would he consider that she was not pulling her weight in the marriage? The boys: would they find her a less interesting person if she did not have a 'proper' job? Her parents: they had already accused her of wasting her education. Her former boss: he felt that she owed it to herself and to the bank to pursue her former career. Her friends: they could not understand her desire to 'bury herself' at home.

  Vivienne had only to consider her children. Her daughter was training to be a nurse and her son was away at university. Although both lived away from home while studying, if the flat was let they would have nowhere to stay during vacations. It would also be the first time Vivienne would have been away from them for so long.

- *Which of those people really have a right to be considered?*
Alison initially felt that all of them had but, after thinking about it a little more, she decided that the only one at this stage was Tim. Her sons were too young to ask and, while everyone else had the right to express an opinion, she had every right to consider or ignore those views. Having made her decision, she spoke to her husband and was delighted to find that he was happy for her to do whatever she wanted. They were fortunate in that they did not need to rely on what she could earn and so it seemed that nothing would stand in her way.

Vivienne's immediate reaction was to say 'no one' but then she felt guilty and wondered whether this made her a bad mother. As she thought it through, however, she decided that she had been the best mother she could for all those years and, now that her children were adult, they could perfectly well fend for themselves during the time she was away.

- *What other aspect of the decision worries you?*
Alison was troubled that she would be considered 'odd' or 'different'. After all, women had struggled for years to be accepted on equal terms with men in the workplace, and here she was throwing away her opportunity. Was there something wrong with her that she did not wish for a career in banking or anything else? Eventually, however, she came to the conclusion that, provided she and Tim were happy, it did not really matter what anyone else thought.

Vivienne's main concern was for her long-term future. What would happen when she came back from her travels? Would she be able to obtain another teaching post? Would she find it difficult to settle down again? What would she do for money?

- *What is the worst outcome you can imagine and what would you do about it should it arise?*
Alison said that she could have made completely the wrong

decision and might find after a short time that she was not happy being at home but had destroyed her chances of ever returning to the bank. As to what she would do, she said she would look for other work, even if it meant going on a training course or starting at the beginning again. She would not be under any great financial pressure and so could spend time finding the right opportunity.

Vivienne's worst possible outcome was that she would dislike the constant travelling and would return home to find that she could not get into her own flat and could not find job. When asked what she would do about it, she said that – as she could not really see how she would not enjoy travelling – she would take her chances on that. She could arrange for her flat to be let on renewable short-term leases so that she would never be homeless for more than a very brief period. She could also put a portion of her savings into the bank so that she had something to live on while looking for a job once she had returned.

- *If you have made provisions for the worst possible scenario, what is now standing in your way?*
  Alison: Nothing.
  Vivienne: Nothing.

——— *Solving shared problems* ———

In many cases, of course, the problems and decisions do not concern one person alone. There are many instances where the wants of two (or more) people are diametrically opposed, and in such cases compromise is necessary. This requires both parties to recognise each other's rights and needs as well as their own. What happens in many cases, however, is that the more aggressive of the two gets his or her own way while the more submissive one gives in at every stage.

You might think that this would result in at least one of them being happy with the outcome but this is not the case. The 'winner' may seem to have got what they want, but unless totally insensitive, will realise that it is at the expense of the other person. The 'loser' will eventually despise him or herself for giving in and will also despise the other person for causing them to do so.

True assertiveness requires a win/win situation where, although neither party may have achieved exactly what they wanted, they have discussed it, understood the other person's point of view and come to a reasoned decision which satisfies both of them.

Opening the lines of communication

Civilised disagreement is not such a bad thing. In fact, it would be a boring world indeed if we all thought, spoke and acted in exactly the same way. But, whereas a difference of opinion is quite healthy, the same cannot be said for bitterness, anger or loss of control. If two parties care about each other – whatever their relationship – they will understand from the outset that compromise may be the only solution.

The most important thing is to open the lines of communication as soon as possible. More problems are often caused by people thinking that they know what the other person feels than by actually discovering and discussing those feelings. Here are a few points to bear in mind:

- Start talking to each other about the problem or the decision as soon as it arises, or you will simply build up the imagined difficulties in your own mind.

- Start by stating your own ideal outcome to the problem, while acknowledging that this may have to be modified in order to accommodate some of the wishes of the other person.

- Be completely honest from the outset. There is no point in half-truths – even for the best possible motive – particularly when the situation is important.

- As you consider the possibilities together, make a written list of the pros and cons of the situation from each point of view. It is interesting to see that compromise is often more easily reached after compiling written notes of this sort, to which you can both refer at will, than after conversations containing inaccurately remembered words and phrases.

- Use combined intuitive powers – we all have them. Take each possible scenario in turn and imagine the outcome resulting from it, in the short and the long-term. How will it affect each of you? Will you be able to cope with that effect? What would make it better? What would make it worse? The more questions you can ask yourselves and the more you listen to each other's answers, the more likely you are to reach a satisfactory compromise.

- If yours is one of those cases where the other person never seems to have the time to listen to what you want to say or to join in the relevant discussion, try to persuade them away from their own environment and on to neutral territory. Perhaps you could go to a coffee shop, a restaurant or some other public place where he or she really has no alternative but to sit there and talk or listen to you.

When compromise is denied

Barbara and Graham had been living together for almost seven years. They had no children, and had long ago decided that they did not want any. Each worked for an extremely large corporation and each was doing very well in their career.

One evening, when Barbara had not been home for long, Graham burst in excitedly. Hugging Barbara, he told her that he had some wonderful news. He had been offered the job of a lifetime! He was being put in charge of the company's new offices in

Edinburgh, which would mean an increase in status and responsibility – and a considerable increase in salary. It was a dream come true!

So excited was Graham, that originally he was not aware of Barbara's hesitancy. But she was devastated. To think that this man with whom she had shared her life for the past seven years – who had seemed to understand and to empathise with her and her dreams – should not even have paused to consider whether this news would be wonderful to her. Of course, she was delighted that the company thought so highly of Graham that they had offered him this position – but what about her? What about her career? She was doing extremely well, too, and knew that she was also in line for promotion. How could she now uproot herself and move to the other end of the country – even if she wanted to?

What hurt her even more was that it had not even occurred to Graham that she might feel this way. He had not come home to tell her of the offer and talk it over with her. Oh, no! He had come home with his mind made up, having decided to accept and having assumed that she would pack her bags and follow him.

Because of all these feelings, Barbara's initial reaction was to become angry. Instead of congratulating Graham, she angrily accused him of being insensitive, selfish and uncaring. Stung, he naturally retaliated by acting in similar fashion.

Once tempers had cooled, they began to calm down and talk about the situation. For Graham the decision was black and white. This was a once-in-a-lifetime offer and he was not about to turn it down. He loved Barbara and wanted to be with her, and, therefore, she would naturally (as he put it) come with him. She was bright enough to be able to find another job in a different part of the country.

Barbara, however, was being pulled in two directions. On the one hand she did love Graham and want to be with him. On the other, even setting aside his lack of sensitivity, why should she give up all that she had worked for to set off to a place where she might or might not get another good job? And even if she did find appropriate work she certainly would be in the position of having to start from lower down the scale and prove herself all over again.

This was one of those very difficult situations with no ideal solution. But, had both these people been prepared to discuss it with a view to reaching some sort of compromise, perhaps the relationship could have been saved. As it turned out, only Barbara was even prepared to talk about it. As far as Graham was concerned, he was going to Edinburgh and Barbara could follow or not as she chose.

Poor Barbara agonised for ages over what she should do. In the end, it was Graham's own obstinacy which split the relationship rather than whether or not she should give up her own job to go with him. She felt that his assumption that he was right and that she must make a choice indicated that he did not think as highly of her as she had believed. He was prepared to abandon their relationship without even discussing the matter. That was what hurt, and it was that which made Barbara decide that a relationship built on such a shaky foundation was not worth uprooting herself for, in case she found herself at the other end of the country with no Graham and no career either.

No-win situations

Meriel's situation was quite different and yet, in the end, she found herself having to be the one who made the final decision. She had been married to Arthur for 16 years and their three children were all away at public school. Arthur was a pillar of the local community – a member of the council, various committees, governing bodies and so on. He was also an extremely wealthy man; they lived in a beautiful home on the edge of town, were members of the tennis and golf clubs and entertained regularly. Meriel, who had married Arthur when she was just 19, had not worked since that time, although she served on various charitable committees.

When I first met Meriel she described her life as 'perfect' – with one exception. Arthur's sexual tastes were very different from her own. He had always shown a preference for somewhat violent sex and this was getting worse.

Convent educated, Meriel had been a virgin when they married and her husband had assured her that this was how sex was supposed to be. He had also made her feel inexperienced and foolish if ever she objected. Now, however, she was older and wiser, and resented having to take part in the kind of sex games her husband favoured.

Meriel had no doubt that her husband loved her. She did not believe he was sexually involved with anyone else. And he certainly did not force his violence upon her if she objected. But he showed his displeasure in other ways. If she complied with his wishes in bed, he was the perfect husband – kind, attentive and loving. If she objected to the inclusion of violence in the sexual act, he desisted but would barely speak to her for days afterwards, spending all his free time on the golf course or out with friends.

Meriel did not know what to do. She knew that Arthur was not going to change and she wanted me to decide for her whether she should stay in the marriage and put up with his behaviour, or whether she should leave. Naturally, I had to tell her that I could not make the decision for her. I could help her as she came to her own conclusions, and I could certainly be supportive whatever conclusion she reached – but that was all.

The problem, as Meriel saw it, was that she had so much to lose. If she left Arthur, she would have far less money and none of the lifestyle privileges to which she had grown accustomed. This would be bound to affect her children, too. Never having had a job and being 36 years old, she did not know what she would do to support herself. And, apart from this one aspect, his sexual proclivities, she did love her husband. If she stayed she could continue with the way of life she enjoyed but either she would have to comply with his sexual wishes or to put up with his indifference.

For Meriel there seemed to be guilt all around. If she left, she would feel guilty for breaking up the family home and distressing her children. If she stayed and complied she would feel guilty for letting herself down but, if she did not, Arthur had the power to make her feel guilty for being 'unnatural' and 'not like other women'.

Whatever decision I would have come to in Meriel's case and

whatever you think she should have done, she finally decided – as she had every right to do – to stay with her husband for the sake of the good life she and her children could have. She told me that she would not allow him to act violently towards her during sex and would put up with his resulting coldness – but whether she did this or not I do not know.

Had Meriel chosen otherwise, we could have gone on together to work on her lack of self-esteem, as it was this which had caused her to allow her husband to act in the way he did in the past and caused her feelings of guilt in the present. In the light of her decision to stay on, all I could do at the time was try and help her become more assertive in all aspects of her life. She did respond well and changed considerably over the next few months, having a greater belief in herself and her own abilities. (See also Chapter Eight).

———— Be true to yourself ————

Whatever decisions you have to face and whatever conclusions you come to, in the end it is always up to you. Once you have made up your mind and when you know you are doing what you consider to be your best at the time, go ahead with your plans. Very few things are cast in stone and there is nothing to say you cannot change direction in the future. What is important is that you are true to yourself and your existing beliefs at each stage.

— 4 —

Learning to
Like Yourself

Do you like yourself? Possibly not, if you are carrying around a
lot of guilt – if you feel that you are far from perfect. But the fact
is that no one is perfect. And that is just as well, because they
would be extremely boring individuals if they were. But, if you
are able to like someone else whom you know not to be perfect,
what is there stopping you liking yourself? Liking yourself, in
spite of your faults, makes sound sense if you are to live your life
fully and enjoyably.

Dr Maxwell Maltz, author of *Psycho-cybernetics* and *The Magic
Power of Self-Image Psychology* says: 'If anyone should be your
friend, it should be you! If you don't like yourself, who will?'

—— *Using your own judgment* ——

You saw in Chapter Two that most of the opinions you hold about
yourself were formed in early childhood – and that you probably
had no choice in how you felt about yourself at the time. But the
moment has come to realise that you – *and only you* – are the one
who chooses whether to continue to hold those opinions now.

Looking back, you may decide that those who instilled those opinions in you were wrong, but even if you feel that they *were* appropriate at the time, that does not make them appropriate now. When you were a child, it may have been appropriate for you to wear mittens threaded on cord through the sleeves of your jacket, as otherwise you would probably have lost them. But you surely would not feel the necessity to do the same thing now. Just as that need has disappeared, so has the need to continue carrying around someone else's opinion of you.

Beware of making negative statements about yourself and allowing repetition to make them valid. Start asking yourself where those statements came from and who instigated them. When you have thought back to who those people were, ask yourself whether they were right or not and, if you think they were, what makes you think that.

Sandra – breaking the mould

'I'm rather shy,' Sandra told me when we first met, 'I'm not very good with people.' She explained that she had never been terribly popular, was always the one in the corner at parties and found it difficult to talk to people. And yet there she was, talking quite easily to me after just 10 minutes acquaintance.

'Oh, that's different,' she said when I mentioned this. 'You're so easy to talk to.' Complimentary as this may have been, she had not had time to discover this when she started chatting freely to me so, I wondered, how had she come to this conclusion. Sandra thought for a moment and then said she thought it was because I was the only person there and I was giving her my full attention. She did not feel she had to compete with anyone else while she was with me.

I asked Sandra to tell me about her present life, and she spoke proudly about her husband, Terry, and her two schoolboy sons. She told me about her job, which involved painting intricate designs on beautiful porcelain, and her hobbies – she played both the piano and the organ. She spoke easily and freely with no hint of shyness.

When I asked her how, if she was so 'bad with people', she had ever managed to get a job – let alone meet and marry a man – she said that was 'different' too. The manager of the porcelain factory was a friend of her father's and, having known Sandra for many years, had invited her to use her artistic skills within the company. As for Terry, he was as quiet as his wife, so he would not have wanted her to be loud and outgoing. 'Do you love him?' I asked. 'Oh, yes,' she replied. 'He's a lovely, gentle and caring man.'

I then asked Sandra why, if she found a quiet and gentle man lovable, should she think that others could not find her lovable, too. And the factory manager must have thought sufficiently highly of her to want her to work for him. He would never have suggested it otherwise.

When I asked Sandra to think back and see if she could remember who it was who first told her that she was shy and awkward with others, her reply was very revealing. She recalled that her parents were outgoing, fun-loving people, always surrounded by friends and the centre of attention wherever they went. They were both members of a local amateur operatic society and their house was always filled with people who had come to rehearse or to enjoy one of the couple's many parties.

Sandra was their only child and on one occasion when she was three or four years of age, they had coached her to stand in front of all these grown-ups and sing, dance or recite for them. Even after all the intervening years, Sandra still blushed as she remembered how awkward and embarrassed she had felt as they looked at her expectantly. Her mind went blank and she could not even remember the words of the nursery rhymes she heard every day. She could still see the look of consternation and disappointment on the faces of her parents as she burst into tears and ran from the room.

From that time onwards her father, who truly loved his little daughter, would shield her from embarrassment by telling the assembled company that Sandra was 'very shy'. His intention was simply to protect her but, of course, as we have already seen, anything which is repeated over and over is eventually accepted as a fact.

Sandra had allowed a label to be attached to her and, because she loved and admired her parents, had assumed that the label must be deserved. In all the intervening years she had not stopped to think that perhaps they were just different in personality. They obviously loved being surrounded by other people with all the noise and exuberance that entails, while she preferred quieter pursuits with one or two friends.

It was only because of her quiet, thoughtful personality that Sandra had attracted the husband she loved and who loved her deeply in return. Terry would never have wanted to share his life with someone who was blatantly extrovert; he was more than happy with her as she was.

Had Sandra been unhappy with her life rather than with her label, things would have been different. But she loved her work, her home and her family. The only thing she found it difficult to come to terms with was that she was not as she believed she 'should' be. Once the 'should' disappeared and she accepted that she had the right to be as she chose, the discontent disappeared and she was able to continue enjoying her life without feeling guilty about her personality.

But what about those people who are not happy in their lives and who really do not like themselves – how are they to change?

—— *Making deliberate changes* ——

The first thing to appreciate is that making deliberate changes is not easy. It is easier by far to stick with what we know than to alter any aspect of ourselves. And yet such conservatism really does not make sound sense. Change is an essential part of progress. A man does not go around wearing the flared trousers and flowery shirts he wore in the early 70s; a woman no longer has the same hair-style or make-up she wore 20 years ago. At some point those people made a conscious decision to change and, in just the same way, you can make a conscious decision to change yourself in whatever way you want.

With decision and perseverance, the new aspects of you can become as comfortable as the old ones were. If you have a parting in your hair, try making it in a different place. For the first few days it may feel unnatural and uncomfortable but eventually you will not even think about it and the new style will have become the one you are used to. A new self-image can be uncomfortable in the beginning, too, but given a little time you will accept it and feel at ease with it.

Change forces you to choose how much control to have over your own life, particularly if you have been clinging to an internal view of yourself created by the words and actions of someone else. Becoming the master of your self-image, and taking control can be a bit frightening – rather like passing your driving test and realising that now you are in sole control of a vehicle which could prove dangerous if misused. However, have you ever heard of anyone handing their certificate back to the examiner and saying that they would prefer to continue driving only with an instructor?

Once you do take control of your own life and attitudes, you are certain to make mistakes along the way. Everyone does. But mistakes serve a great purpose in that they show us what to do – or not do – in the future. If you make a cake which fails to rise, drive your car into a lamppost or fall over when learning to skate, you don't shut down that aspect of your life and refuse to cook, drive or skate again. You look into the possible reasons for the mistake: too few eggs, too little use of the rear view mirror or leaning too far forward – and learn how not to repeat them.

If you try to change some aspect of yourself in a positive way and it does not work out, that does not make you a failure or a bad person. Examine the possible reasons why it has not worked. Perhaps it was due to unfortunate external circumstances, an error of judgment on your part or a failure to take consequences into account. Having decided why you failed, reorganise your plans accordingly.

Start small

Of one thing you can be sure; if you continue to think as you have always thought and act as you have always acted, you will continue to see the results you have always seen. If those results do not satisfy you, then you *must* change the way you think and act. If something is not working for you, do what you can to change it. If that something is the way you think about yourself, then learn to alter your self-image.

This may involve trial and error but many worthwhile objectives do. Remember to start small, and have patience. There may be a number of aspects of yourself you do not like, but you cannot change them all at once. Decide on the one which matters most to you, and ask yourself the following questions:

- *What is the character trait I would most like to change?* Be as specific as possible. There is no point in vaguely telling yourself that you are 'not nice', 'stupid', or 'inferior'. In what way does the characteristic show itself? Find some actual examples.

- *Is this really a failing?* Remember how Sandra based her view of what she should be like on someone else's more extrovert personality and opinion. Ask yourself whether the character trait you wish to change is really bad, or whether it is just different from that of some other people – particularly those who are close to you or who were around you when you were growing up.

- *In what way would I like to be different?* There is no point in deciding what you do not like about yourself if you cannot also decide on the way in which you would like to be different.

- *How would this difference show itself in my everyday life?* Would it be visible to other people, or would you be the only one to be aware of the change in you? Imagine you were writing a job description and describe how, if you were to alter this characteristic, you would look, act and speak differently.

53

Would there be any negative result of making this change? If Sandra had decided to alter her personality to that of her mother or father, and had she been able to do so, she would have lost more than she gained. Terry would no longer have felt comfortable with her and might even have found it too difficult to continue sharing his life with someone so different. She might have grown discontented with the job which so suited her temperament and personality. She might even have acted towards her children as her parents did towards her and – even though their motives were good – their words and actions had caused her years of believing that she was inferior.

Only after carefully considering all of these questions can you make up your mind to make a specific change and decide how to go about it.

Finding a role model

One of the ways you can make the change you have chosen is to observe someone else who seems to be the type of person you want to become. I do not mean that you should slavishly imitate another person. We are all different and this is how it should be; to lose your individuality would be a mistake. But notice what your role model does or says which is different from the way you act or speak.

Suppose, for example, you wish that you were a more demonstrative person. Perhaps you feel very deeply for other people but are not very good at showing your emotions. How can you make it obvious that you care without acting in a falsely gushing manner?

Look around you at people you know, and select as your role model someone who is able to show genuine affection for those closest to her. Watch her and see what she does and how she does it. Notice the way in which she greets close friends and her family, and the way she takes her leave of them. Does she kiss them or hug them? Observe her body language during a conversation with these people. See how she leans towards them as she speaks and perhaps puts out a hand and touches them on the arm. These are the sort of patterns to build into your own body-language although obviously you will only use them when the affectionate feeling is there in the first place.

Acting differently in this way may feel awkward at first, but so does wearing a new pair of shoes. Just as the shoes eventually become flexible and comfortable, so, too, will your new behaviour. And, as you become aware of the pleasure you are bringing to those around you, this will make it even easier and more natural for you to continue in the new way.

Common needs

If you are dissatisfied with your present self and want to make some changes, it might help to bear in mind that we all have certain needs in common:

- *The need to be loved* There are many kinds of love; not just the man/woman relationship. If you take 'love' to mean being important to someone else, you will see that it applies just as much to love between parent and child, family members or close friends. And love is something we all desire and need. To know that you really matter to another person is a wonderful thing. If you feel that it's wonderful, be sure to let the other person see that you do. When you know how good it makes you feel, do what you can to help someone else feel this way too.

  As a counsellor, I have become so used to hearing people say such things as, 'Well, I don't have to tell her. She knows I love her', or 'Because my mother never told me so, I didn't realise she loved me until I was adult'. How sad that so many people unwittingly deprive others of something they could so easily give, and which would make a vast difference to how they feel about themselves.

- *The need to feel that we matter* The saddest comment I have heard recently was when a patient told me that, if she died in her sleep that very night, it wouldn't make any difference to anyone because she didn't matter. Yet we all matter, even those who have no close family members to tell them so. Each of us can choose to play a part in making the world a better place and, by doing so, become a truly important person. Think back on the ways you have changed something in the world. Whether you planted a tree, were kind to someone in need, bore a child, helped a neighbour or donated items to a charity shop – you have *done something*. The something does not have to have been enormous; the fact is that it made a difference in some way. If each person were to do something positive, however small, think of the changes which could be brought about. How do you feel now, knowing that you have made a difference? Good, I hope; you deserve to. Because now you know that you do matter.

- *The need to exercise some control over our lives* Whether we want to control the sameness or to control the changes, knowing that we are making that decision brings a sense of security. And it is only the inwardly secure person who is capable of making deliberate changes because we all know that change carries with it an element of risk. What if things don't turn out as you hope? Change involves courage – including the courage to say, 'Well, that didn't work out too well, so I need to change course again.'

- *The need to enjoy ourselves* The world can be a serious place, with problems related to work and to personal life. But this doesn't mean that you are not entitled to have some fun too, doing something which may be totally non-productive but which you thoroughly enjoy. If you are someone who never seems to find time for personal pleasure, this could be an important area of your life you need to re-plan.

—— *Deciding what you don't want* ——

If you know you would like to change but are not quite sure in what direction, try looking at things from the opposite viewpoint. You may not know what you want but I am certain there are things that you know you *don't* want. Being as spontaneous as possible, make a list now of three things about yourself that you no longer want.

When a patient of mine named Gail made her list it read:

I do not want:
1 To lose my temper so often.
2 To be doing the same job in five years time.
3 To be on the committee.

That list surprised even Gail herself – which is the benefit of writing it spontaneously as opposed to thinking too hard about it. She knew that she had a tendency to flare up at little things and that she would prefer not to do so. She had often moaned about her job, which was safe and fairly well-paid but dull and uninteresting – but she had never actually considered leaving it. As for the committee, she had been approached by a friend who worked for a fund-raising organisation to see whether she would be prepared to become a local committee member. Gail wasn't particularly keen but she had not realised that she felt so strongly about it. But, having come to that conclusion, she decided that she would refuse the opportunity even though it would be hard to tell her friend that she was turning it down.

When Gail kindly but firmly turned down the opportunity to join the committee she was pleasantly surprised to find that her friend accepted her decision with equanimity. Because we do dislike saying no, we tend to believe that, if we do, other people's reaction will be aggressive but usually this is not the case.

With regard to Gail's wish to be in a different job, naturally that was not something she could deal with overnight. But, having once stated that it was her ambition to make a change, she had a starting point from which to work. She could think about the type of work she would find fulfilling and stimulating, and set about looking for it or, if necessary, find a way to train for such work.

Like Gail, once you have identified precisely what it is that you do *not* want, you should find it easier to list what you do want.

―――――― *Keeping a diary* ――――――

Another way of gaining insight into yourself and your personality, is to keep a diary in which you can record your experiences over a period of, say, three weeks. No-one else need ever see this record, so be honest about what happened during that period and how you felt about it – break it down into what was good and what was bad.

If there was anything during that three-week period which made you feel bad, try analysing what it was and why it affected you in this way. (If it was a 'one-off' instance, you do not need to take it into account; it is when you come across the kind of thing which happens too often in your life that you need to think about it.) Ask yourself the following questions:

● What was the event?

● In what way did it make you feel bad?

● Is this the type of thing which occurs frequently in your life?

● If so, can you think of a way of avoiding it?

● What aspect of yourself or your way of life can you change so that this particular event is less likely to occur in the future?

Then analyse the situation which made you feel good, stop and ask yourself why it did so and what you can do to have that good feeling more often.

- What was the situation?

- In what way did it make you feel good?

- Is this the type of thing which occurs frequently in your life?

- If not, can you think of a way of ensuring that it does?

- What aspect of yourself or your way of life can you change so that this particular situation and the feeling it carries with it is likely to occur more often in the future?

—— *Changing negative situations* ——

Some negative situations are extremely difficult to avoid. In many instances, the fact that you find them negative causes you to blame yourself – whether or not this is justified – and thus induces a sense of guilt for not being able to cope better. Here, too, a little analysis and planning for the future can be helpful, as Helen discovered.

Helen shared an office with two other young women – Marsha and Jacqueline. Both were pleasant but, while Marsha would quietly get on with her work, Jacqueline was always talking – often about nothing in particular. It seemed to Helen that whenever she was concentrating on a particularly tricky piece of work her thoughts would be interrupted by Jacqueline's chatter.

It wasn't that Helen didn't enjoy talking with her two colleagues but, because the office was so busy, it was easier to restrict such conversations to coffee break or lunch time. Only Jacqueline didn't seem to realise this and she would perch on Helen's desk, disrupting the papers lying there, and start to regale her with details of her social life.

When this happened Helen would say nothing but would concentrate on her work, hoping that Jacqueline would stop talking and go away. But this never happened, and eventually Helen would lose her temper and shout at Jacqueline to leave her alone. Only then did she stop and, looking hurt, return to her own desk.

This left Helen feeling extremely guilty. If Jacqueline had been an unpleasant person, she would not have felt bad about shouting at her. But the young woman was kind and friendly – even if she was irritating.

Helen realised that something had to be done if the three of them were to continue to work amicably together. Marsha didn't want to become involved, Jacqueline herself did not realise how annoying she could be – so it was up to Helen to work out what to do. She asked herself the following questions in order to clarify just what changes she wanted.

- *What is wrong with the current situation?* Jacqueline's incessant chatter at inappropriate times was preventing any of them getting on efficiently with their work.

- *How was she handling the situation at present?* By saying and doing nothing until her patience was eroded and she lost her temper with Jacqueline.

- *How did she then feel?* Guilty because she felt that she was being unkind to someone who did not really deserve it. Then resentful towards Jacqueline for making her feel guilty and towards Marsha for doing nothing.

- *What outcome did she want?* To be able to get on with her work. To make Jacqueline realise that she was interfering. Not to hurt the other woman's feelings. To be on good terms with both Marsha and Jacqueline. To persuade Jacqueline that social chit-chat was best reserved for social times of day, such as lunch hour or coffee break.

- *How was she to achieve her aims?* Helen realised that there was little point remonstrating with Jacqueline when she was in full flow. Helen therefore resolved to take Jacqueline to one side and – more difficult – to make her listen.

The one word which tends to stop anyone who is in mid-conversation is the sound of their own name – repeated if necessary. So the next time Jacqueline interrupted her, Helen used it sharply: 'Jacqueline. . .Jackie!' There was a sudden silence as the other woman looked at her expectantly. Seizing the moment, Helen told Jacqueline she had something very important to say to her and asked her if they could meet at tea-time in the café next door.

This achieved two things: it stopped the flow of Jacqueline's chatter and it aroused her curiosity, so that when she and Helen met that afternoon, she remained silent, anxious to discover what her colleague had to say.

Helen chose her words carefully. She explained to Jacqueline that she enjoyed talking to her but that she found it difficult to concentrate on her work when constantly interrupted. Jacqueline was quite shocked; she had not realised that this was how she came across to others. She told Helen that she never had any intention of disrupting either her or Marsha's work but had simply wanted to pass on what she thought would be considered interesting snippets of information. Of course, she wouldn't do it again.

Human nature being what it is, Helen knew that, despite Jacqueline's best intentions, she was likely to forget her promise and habit would cause her to act in the same way in the future. So they agreed that, if this happened, Helen would simply interrupt and remind her that she was chattering and Jacqueline would not take offence but would leave the conversation for a later time. And that is what happened.

By asking herself the right questions and working out an appropriate course of action, Helen had achieved all she wanted.

She put an end to the constant interruptions without hurting Jacqueline's feelings or causing disharmony in the office. And, just as important, she had put an end to the feelings of guilt she had previously been suffering.

— 5 —

When an Apology is Due

We've already seen that much of the guilt many people experience only exists because of the actions or attitudes of other people in the past. However, because we are all fallible, there are bound to be occasions when we *have* said or done something of which we later feel ashamed, and about which we believe that we should feel guilty.

Guilt, of course, is a completely useless emotion; in itself it achieves nothing. Feeling guilty does not make you a better person or prevent you from making mistakes (whether similar or different) in the future. All it does is cause you to become depressed, sly or aggressive – depending upon your personal reactions.

Guilt is only the starting-point. It can be helpful in that it brings home to you the wrong that you said or did. However, it is what you do from that point onwards which is important, and which has a bearing on how you live the rest of your life and how you feel about yourself.

Confession – thought to be good for the soul – is pointless unless, at the same time, you resolve to ensure that circumstances do not repeat themselves. Even punishment serves little purpose if all it does is make the guilty party feel that he or she has 'paid for' any mistakes and so is starting again from scratch.

You have an advantage over such people. Whatever led you to

do it, you have made a deliberate choice to read this book. You are therefore sensitive enough to realise that guilt can be a real problem in your life and you have chosen to learn how you can make changes.

———— *Go easy on yourself* ————

The first thing to realise is that we all make mistakes as we journey through life; you do not have to be the only saint among mere mortals. Some of your mistakes will have been major ones and some trivial. Some will have resulted from carelessness, others from deliberate wrong-doing. Whatever they were and however they arose, the fact that you now want to put matters right shows that you have learned and evolved as a result of them.

We are always far harder on ourselves than we are on other people. If you know that someone you love and care for has done something wrong but now sincerely regrets the deed, you will usually give them another chance. Why, then, is it so difficult to do the same for yourself? Why should you have to be any more 'perfect' than anyone else?

— *Guilt and obsessional behaviour* —

The person suffering from guilt does not always realise that this is the root cause of other problems.

For example, when Sarah came to see me it was for help in dealing with obsessional behaviour. An intelligent and articulate woman, she was fanatical about cleanliness. She felt compelled to wash her hands innumerable times throughout the day. When her children came in from school, they had to change all their clothes and those they had been wearing were washed immediately. When they got up in the morning, all nightwear also went straight into the machine. As Sarah had five children, this meant that her washing machine was in use night and day, while she herself became exhausted as a result of all the effort involved in this and her daily ritual of cleaning and polishing.

I asked Sarah to tell me something about herself. She explained that she was very happily married to Bob. Their lives revolved around each other and the children, to whom they were devoted. Bob had a good job and the family had no financial problems. He was even being very patient about her obsessional washing, although Sarah knew that he found it worrying and wanted her to seek help.

An only child, Sarah had attended a convent school where she received a good education and did well in her exams. She had chosen not to go to university but had spent two years at a polytechnic before working as a secretary until the birth of her first child. Since that time she had not worked outside the home.

An early taboo

The clue to the cause of the problem came when Sarah was talking about her school and the nuns who taught her. They had been fair though strict, but sex education was limited to biological explanation and the opinion that women should be prepared to endure the sexual act in order to conceive children. Although Sarah laughed a little when she told me this, she blushed as she said that she and Bob had a wonderful sex life which brought them both joy.

I decided to pursue this line, using hypnosis and analysis. It soon became obvious that Sarah had a great sense of inner guilt because she enjoyed her sexual relationship with her husband so much when she had been told that this was not how she should feel. Under hypnosis, she recalled one of the teachers at the convent equating sex with being 'dirty'. It was this remark which had sown the seeds of her later obsessional washing – as if she was trying to wash away her guilt for being a 'dirty person'.

I am not here criticising convent education, only the particular sister responsible for sex education at that particular school. She may have been acting in what she saw as the best interests of the girls in her class, but she actually laid the foundations for any number of future neuroses.

———————— *Self-analysis* ————————

If *you* are suffering from a sense of guilt, ask yourself whether it exists because you did or said something wrong or whether your behaviour or words simply were not in accord with what someone else believed to be right. In the latter event, you can let go of the guilt for ever. There is no reason why you should condemn yourself because someone else held different views from yours. Indeed, they may even have forgotten all about their words while they continue to fester inside you.

When you are at fault

Let us suppose that, having considered that point, you decide that you really do deserve to feel guilty because of something you did or said. It is time to look at your intention on that occasion. Intention makes a great deal of difference.

If I walk past you in a crowded area and accidentally step hard on your toe, it will hurt. The physical pain will be the same if I deliberately stamp on your foot. But my intention will be completely different – as will be the way in which you react. Your first instinct may be the same in either case – you might yell with pain, call me a clumsy fool and push me away. But, as the pain and the anger subside, you will realise that, in the first instance, I had no intention of hurting you and you are unlikely to bear any long-term grudge. Your feelings towards me and your subsequent reactions are likely to be quite different, however, if you realise that I deliberately hurt you.

In the same way, when you look back upon things you may

have done wrong in the past, you should take into account your intention at the time. However bad it was, however much it hurt another person, if it was an accident then, having apologised and done what you can to make up for it, there is little point in continuing to beat yourself with an emotional whip.

Perhaps what you did was accidental but arose through unforeseen circumstances or carelessness, as opposed to malice. For example, very few people intend to knock anyone down while driving a car but it happens. It may have been caused by something over which you had no control – a mechanical failure in the vehicle perhaps. Perhaps it was due to criminal carelessness, such as driving when you had been drinking over the limit. In many instances, however, such an accident results from a human fallibility – such as a momentary lapse of attention. We all know that this should not happen – but we also know that it does. And you are bound to feel very guilty but, unless you decide to pay closer attention in the future, the guilt in itself will achieve nothing but further harm – this time, to you.

Dealing with actual guilt

There are three principal stages involved when dealing with events causing genuine feelings of guilt.

1 *Apologise.* Where possible, this should be done at the time or as soon afterwards as can be. If tempers where high and you said something you later regret, you might not realise until you calm down that you need to apologise. If the person you have hurt will not speak to you, try writing to them and explaining how sorry you feel.

   In some cases an apology is not possible. You may have lost touch with the person involved – or they may even have died. In such instances all you can do is realise that you do regret what happened and that you would apologise if it were at all possible.

2 *Put things right if you can.* Sometimes this is easy to do, some-

times it is difficult and sometimes it is impossible. If you hurt someone's feelings with harsh words or if you take something which does not belong to you, there are ways of making amends. It is not quite so straightforward if you have done them physical harm or if you have destroyed something which was theirs, but you may be able to find an appropriate way of compensating for what you did.

More serious: how do you put things right if you have done someone permanent harm – whether physical or emotional? And what do you do if that person is no longer alive? Sometimes in such circumstances, the only positive thing you can do is to make the necessary changes in yourself, your attitudes and behaviour so that you would never do such a thing again.

3 *Learn from your mistakes.* If your past words or deeds brought about a situation which caused you to feel guilty, at least you have the advantage of knowing what *not* to do in the future. Use the experience as an object lesson and it will not have been entirely negative. From the very beginning of our lives we learn by what we do wrong. The small child learning to walk will fall over many times but she will soon learn to adjust her balance so that she does not. Young people go through many phases when it comes to handling emotional relationships; by making mistakes and learning from the outcome they can find out how to behave in such a way that their later emotional life is far more settled.

Julie – a case of self-punishment

Guilt which is not handled in this way, that is, learning from mistakes and then taking a positive view, can cause you to inflict all kinds of self-punishment. Julia is a case in point. She originally came to see me because she wanted to lose weight. A young and attractive woman, she had put on more than three stone over the previous two years and this excess weight was making her unhappy.

The normal hypnotic techniques I use to help those trying to lose weight had no effect whatsoever and it became apparent that Julia's problem was far greater than simply over-eating. I asked her to tell me a little more about herself – and, almost with a sense of relief, she gradually unburdened herself.

She had been married to Peter for nearly eleven years and they had two young sons, both now at school. A little over three years earlier Julia had begun a relationship with a work colleague, Mike. She described this to me as 'more than an affair', emphasising that she and Mike were very much in love. They had continued seeing each other for about six months, managing to keep the whole thing secret from Peter and from Mike's wife and family. At one point they had even contemplated leaving their respective partners and setting up home together, but had decided that the hurt to both families would be too great. Eventually, they concluded that the only thing to do was to end their own relationship as it was putting a great strain on them both.

Mike applied for, and obtained, a position with a company in the United States and, after a parting which was painful and distressing for both of them, he and his family left England to live in Boston. He and Julia decided that it would be best for them to have no future contact and she stayed in her marriage with Peter whom she still loved – although not with the same degree of passion she had felt for Mike.

A weight on her mind

It was after this that Julia began to put on weight. She was not aware of great changes in her eating habits in the initial stages. But as the pounds piled on she became so miserable about it that she did then begin to eat more than previously. And so the weight continued to rise and she felt herself trapped on a never-ending spiral.

Peter had never known about his wife's affair, and he continued to be very happy with his marriage and his family life. Julia had also become happier and was now horrified to think how close she had come to throwing away the love of her husband and hurting the children she adored. And still her weight continued to increase.

There were two principal reasons for Julia's weight gain and these were:

- She felt dreadfully guilty for having betrayed Peter's trust – all the more so because Peter had not discovered the truth and so still had complete faith in his wife. Consciously and subconsciously, Julia felt that she deserved to be punished and, when this punishment was obviously not going to come from the outside, she had to find some inner way of creating it. Thus she had begun to gain weight rapidly – something she hated and yet which, at a deep inner level, satisfied her need for punishment.

- Julia was not by nature a fickle person and, looking back on the affair, she could not understand how she had ever allowed herself to be drawn into such a liaison. Her logical mind told her that she would never permit such a situation to arise again and that, even if tempted, she would be strong and remain faithful to her husband. Her deep inner voice, however – the one which so successfully undermines self-esteem – kept telling her that someone who could stray once could do so again. To prevent this happening, Julia's subconscious had caused her to gain weight rapidly so that she would become so unattractive that no one would ever want to have a relationship with her again. Not being tempted, she would have no reason to be unfaithful.

As it happened, Julia was a very pretty woman and even the extra weight did not make her unattractive, but in her subconscious mind she *felt* that it did and therefore believed herself to be protected from future temptation.

During our sessions together, Julia worked through the various stages of the guilt she was experiencing and, by forgiving herself, allowed the ghosts of the past to be laid. On letting go of the guilt from which she had suffered for so long, she no longer had the need to inflict punishment on herself and over the next few months her excess weight disappeared.

To confess – or not

In cases where you have done something wrong but no one else has discovered that fact, you have to decide whether you should confess or whether it would be better to remain silent. These are the points to be considered:

- *Will confession do more harm than good?* Had Julia told Peter all about her affair, it would have caused him great anguish and have achieved nothing. The relationship with Mike was over and he had gone far away. If Peter had been told, his trust in Julia might have been permanently destroyed, thereby ruining any chance they might have had for happiness in the future and possibly causing great distress to their children.

  Each person must decide for him of herself whether to confess to past misdemeanours. If, as in Julia's case, no purpose would be served by owning up, you then have to ask yourself:

- *Are you capable of remaining silent for ever?* If there is a danger that at some time in the future you are likely to blurt out the truth, it would be better to choose your moment carefully and then, as gently and reassuringly as possible, to explain what you have done. Remember that fear is an extremely destructive emotion (see Chapter One), and you do not want to spend the rest of your life being fearful in case some past misdemeanour comes to light.

- *Taking into account any other people who know – or who might know – of your secret, are they to be trusted?* If you feel that someone else might betray you, it would be better for you to tell the truth first. You can ensure that it is really the truth rather than someone else's idea of it, and that you can explain the situation. You can also give assurances about the future – something which is extremely difficult in the face of angry accusation.

71

Some special cases

In some cases, of course, it is essential to tell the truth. If you have insurance policies, you could find them nullified if you have not been completely honest on the application forms. Even if your honesty means you have to pay a slightly higher premium, what is the point of paying any premium at all if you find at a crucial time the company refuses to pay out because they have discovered a falsehood on the original application form?

Choosing to remain silent

If this is your considered decision and there are cases where this would seem to be appropriate – it is even more important for you to work through personal understanding and personal forgiveness. Failure to do this could cause changes in you such as the one which Julia suffered. Your self-image could sink to such a level that you become depressed or your insecurity might turn you into a more aggressive personality than you previously were. To avoid this, there are several stages to work through:

1 *Consider the event itself and, without deceiving yourself, decide just how terrible it was.* Many people go through life inwardly chastising themselves for past deeds which were foolish rather than dreadful. But guilt has caused these events to become magnified in the imagination until they become enormous crimes. It is very important, therefore, to be aware of the reality of the situation and to put it in proportion with regard to your life and that of others. Even a single lapse into dishonesty is not something to be proud of but, if you know that it really was an isolated incident and that you are never likely to do such a thing again, there is no point in punishing yourself for the rest of your life.

2 *Work at forgiving yourself.* It is usually far harder to do this than it is to forgive other people or, indeed, than it is for other people to forgive you. Ask yourself what will be achieved if

you never forgive yourself. Will you change what happened? You might think that you will prevent yourself lapsing again in the future but you can do this just as well by making a decision and, if necessary, altering the way you have been going about things. Remind yourself of the damage which might be done if you do not forgive yourself. You might change in such a way that you cause distress either to yourself or to those about whom you care most – and, because they will not even understand why this is happening, they will be likely to blame themselves for the difference in you, perhaps thinking that you no longer care for them.

3 *Realise that you are permitted to fail now and then.* No one is perfect; no one glides through life without doing anything wrong. The difference is that some people are able to look on having failed in some way as part of the learning process of life. They pick themselves up and go on, making a conscious decision not to make the same mistake again. Others, however, believe that having failed makes them a failure – not the same thing at all.

When you were learning to walk, you frequently fell over. When learning to drive a car, initially you will have made all kinds of errors. If you have learned to swim, you will have swallowed a considerable amount of water in the process. None of these things prevented you from eventually succeeding because you did not believe that they made you a complete failure. At that time, you did not say to yourself, 'Oh well, I'll just have to crawl on all fours for the rest of my life', 'It's the bus for me from now on', or 'I'll have to give up all hope of learning to swim'. No, you persevered, learning from what you did wrong and adapting your actions accordingly. Surely you can do the same sort of thing now.

5 *Having forgiven yourself and decided not to do the same thing again – let it go!* It is now part of your past and not your present or future. You can only cause yourself distress by concentrating on something you once did. In the same way that

73

someone who has given up smoking must learn to think of themselves as a 'non-smoker' rather than an 'ex-smoker' if they are to succeed, you must learn to think of yourself as the person you want to be rather than the one you previously were.

— *More sinned against than sinning* —

Some people have such submissive personalities that they always assume that they are in the wrong. And, of course, there is always an aggressive person around to reinforce their beliefs! Aggression, even if only verbal, is a form of bullying and is a clear indication of the aggressor's inner insecurity. Someone who is secure and confident in themselves does not see the need to behave aggressively towards anyone else. But, just as a bully will unerringly seek out the timid child in the school playground, the aggressor will soon find the most submissive person in his or her vicinity and pick on them. If you need aggression to bolster a shaky ego, you will not risk trying it on someone who might answer back or stand up to you.

Ask yourself whether you are an excessively submissive person. Do any of the following apply *regularly* to you (don't worry if they are only the case on odd occasions – we all have some bad days)?

- I constantly find myself apologising to others.

- I always fall in with other people's plans.

- I can't say 'no'.

- If someone shouts at me, I become very distressed.

- I believe that everyone else is better/more skilled/more efficient than I am.

- I tend to speak very quietly.

- I find it hard to make and maintain eye contact.

- I have nervous habits, such as biting my fingernails or playing with my hair.

- I would rather do something myself than ask someone else to do it.

- I always take criticism to heart.

- If someone pays me a compliment I cannot accept it (and usually make some negative remark).

If several of the above statements apply to you, you need to work on developing more assertiveness in general. A submissive person is always going to see as enormous any mistake he or she makes and will usually find it extremely difficult to grant self-forgiveness. Learn how to say 'no' without being aggressive. Believe in your own worth and remember – you are a terrific person!

I deliberately have not dealt in this chapter with the very small things which cause us to feel temporarily guilty – such as forgetting an anniversary, scraping the car or breaking a vase. Although we would prefer not to, we all do all these things from time to time and the guilt is usually comparatively short-lived.

By learning how to handle our guilt and regret for the more serious problems in life, we can put our past behind us and find peace of mind for the future.

— 6 —

Resisting Manipulation by Others

In the previous chapter, we dealt with instances where you had instigated and perpetuated feelings of guilt yourself. But what about those occasions when someone else induces in you a sense of guilt – how should you cope with that?

Remember: no one has the power to make you feel guilty unless you permit them to do so. Even when someone sets out to manipulate you and create a sense of guilt in you in order to achieve their own ends, they can only succeed if you help them by thinking continually about their words until you convince yourself that they *must* be right – whatever your logical mind might tell you.

Choosing how to respond

The first part of the process of coping with outside influence is to become aware of it when it occurs. You can then choose how to respond: you might decide to give in to manipulatively-phrased requests or you might prefer to refuse them. But, whichever course you follow, it will be because you have elected to do so rather than been made to feel guilty about it.

To illustrate this point, let's take a fairly common and not too important scenario that is probably repeated in households all over the world. Margot is approached by her 15-year-old daughter Rosie. Rosie has been invited to a party and wants to borrow Margot's new silk shirt. There are several approaches Rosie might try, all of which are aimed at making Margot feel guilty:

- I haven't anything to wear.

- You don't give me enough pocket money to buy any decent clothes.

- Everyone else will be wearing something new.

- Don't you care about how I look?

- It's not a very big thing to ask, is it?

I am sure you can readily invent several more variations on this theme for yourself.

Now Margot may decide that she does not want Rosie to borrow her silk shirt. Perhaps the girl has been careless with her mother's clothes in the past, or perhaps once she has borrowed something it never seems to be returned. Whatever the reason, once she has refused the request, Margot should put the whole episode out of her mind. This is not always made easy by teenage daughters who are capable of running through a gamut of emotions of which any classical actor would be proud.

On the other hand, if Margot decides to lend her silk shirt to her daughter, it should be because she *chooses* to do so and not because she has succumbed to one or more of the manipulative phrases. This does not mean that she is being weak by 'giving in'. She is simply making a decision and following through with action.

—— *Deeper emotional blackmail* ——

But what of the deeper emotional blackmail which is also unfortunately all too common? Think of the phrase 'if you loved me'. That must be one of the most manipulative phrases in existence. 'If you loved me you would buy it for me', 'If you loved me you would take me out tonight', 'If you loved me you'd marry me'. The person saying 'if you loved me' is almost always saying these things to someone who really does love them but there is always the danger that the love could be seriously marred – or even destroyed altogether – if emotions are played upon too often in this way.

Has it ever happened to you? Can you recall a time when someone said to you, 'If you really loved me you would . . .' Even if you acceded to the request, how did you feel afterwards? If you realised that you were being manipulated, you were probably not too happy with yourself for giving in. If you were unaware of what was going on, you may have resented the other person for doubting the strength of your love. Not a good feeling in either case.

Then there are the subtle phrases, such as 'don't worry about me. You go out and enjoy yourself'. 'Don't worry about me – I'll be all right.' What is that really saying? The underlying meaning is, 'I can't stop you going out and, although I shall be fine, I want you to feel guilty about not taking me with you.' This is more insidious – and often much more effective – than sulking or insisting on being taken along. Because, of course, if you do go without them, their words will echo inside your head and you will feel guilty.

There is an old joke told about the mother who buys her adult son two sweaters for his birthday – a red one and a green one. Thanking her effusively, he rushes upstairs and immediately puts on the red one. When he comes, down, his mother takes one look at him and says: 'What's the matter – don't you like the green one I bought you?' Instant guilt!

Con-men play on the fact that they can make you feel guilty.

There have been instances in recent years of pseudo students or charity collectors knocking at the doors of householders and trying to sell them goods, the proceeds from which ostensibly go to help the homeless or to enable the student to complete his studies. Unfortunately these confidence tricksters do nothing to further the cause of many genuine organisations who do their best to raise funds this way. Not only is there less money to go around but, once householders suspect that they have been conned, they will be less likely to give anything in the future.

The same is true about beggars in the streets and at the railway station. Setting aside for a moment the question of whether in the western world today anyone should be forced to beg or sleep rough in order to survive, people who are kind and compassionate enough to help those less fortunate than themselves are less likely to do so after hearing tales of 'beggars' driving home in new cars or 'borrowing' a couple of young children to help them plead their cause. These people too are intent on making you feel guilty – for having when apparently they have not.

— *High motivation — low sensitivity* —

Sometimes those intent on making you feel guilty are doing so because they think it is the right thing to do. Some teachers and some parents believe that they will encourage children to do better by seeming to be disappointed in their efforts. Perhaps this works with some children, although I would think it only does so in the short-term. In the majority of cases, it creates a sense of guilt at having let down the person they have been trying so hard to please. The result is likely to be that, even if they try even harder in the future, nervousness may make them perform even less well. So, far from achieving what they wanted, the adult will have discouraged the child so much that poorer results still are likely to be the outcome. This, in turn, leads to a sense of failure and a lessening of self-esteem which can last a lifetime.

If similar criticism is levelled at the child who knows that she had really done her best – whatever the results – the same outcome is likely, though possibly for a different reason.

When Joanna was at school she attended classes in basic science. Her teacher was extremely knowledgeable but not very skilled at holding the attention of a class of 13-year-olds. Bored, Joanna simply sat at the back of the class and did her history homework instead of paying attention to the lessons. The following year the class had a new science teacher who made the lessons far more participative and interesting for the pupils. But Joanna had not acquired in the first year the basic knowledge needed for her to understand what was going on. She made up her mind that she really wanted to know more about the subject and worked extremely hard for the end of year exam, but, despite all her efforts, she failed it. When the teacher handed back her paper, he berated her in front of the class, criticising her for 'not doing any work in preparation for the exam'. When Joanna tried to explain that she had worked, he called her a liar.

That was it for Joanna. She *knew* how hard she had worked before the exam and if she was not going to be believed she just would not bother in the future. She gave up the study of all science subjects at the first possible opportunity. And all because of the unthinking attitude of one teacher who thought he would make her feel guilty so that she would work harder in future.

—— *Trading on past favours* ——

Some people will use the fact that they have done you a favour in the past to manipulate you for ever afterwards. When you do not fall in with their wishes they will remind you, directly or obliquely, that you are in their debt, and your ensuing guilt is likely to make you do what they ask. The fact is, that whether that person has put themselves out for you on a single occasion or whether it is a case of 'after all I've done for you', no one has the right to manipulate you in this manner. After all, if the original good deeds did not come from the heart, they were not really good deeds.

—— *Living up to expectations* ——

It is difficult enough, saying 'no' to one person with whom you share an emotional bond. When the whole family puts you under pressure it takes real self-confidence to withstand them. Take Paul, for instance.

Paul's family were all members of the legal profession. His mother and father were barristers, his grandfather was head of a firm of solicitors and his uncle was a circuit judge. It had always been assumed, therefore, that Paul was bound to go into the legal profession, too. Indeed, his parents often spoke of this eventuality to friends, colleagues and family.

The trouble was that no one had ever thought to ask Paul what he wanted. And he didn't want to be a lawyer. He wanted to study music. He had played both piano and organ from a very early age and composed pieces which had been performed by himself and others. His family were proud of his obvious talent but they looked on his music as no more than a 'pleasant hobby', and went on assuming that he would become a lawyer. His grandfather spoke of him joining the family firm while his mother and father discussed which chambers he might join.

For a long time Paul remained silent about his real hopes and ambitions. He loved his parents and knew they wanted only the best for him, so he did not feel able to tell them that their only child did not want to follow in the family footsteps. Eventually, however, he reached a point in his studies where he had to make some long-term decisions and it became essential to make his own wishes clear. Summoning all his courage, Paul faced his parents and explained that he wanted to study music as a career. When they finally understood that he was serious, his parents made it painfully clear that they were disappointed and felt that he had let them – and the rest of the family – down.

Paul was left with two options. Either he could give way to his parents' wishes and study to become a lawyer – which would make him unhappy. Or he could pursue his own ambition and study music – in which case he would feel guilty about letting his parents down. He was trapped in a no-win situation.

Had Paul been more assertive he would have taken the latter course but he was young and he was used to doing as his parents wished. So he gave up thoughts of music as a career and settled down to study law. After qualifying and joining the family firm, however, he knew that he had made a mistake and, being older and more inclined to make his own decisions, he applied for, and obtained, a scholarship to the Royal College of Music.

Fortunately for Paul, he had eventually reached a stage where he had the courage to follow his own path. But it would have been so easy for him to allow guilt to push him in a direction he did not want to go, possibly turning him into an unhappy and embittered man.

—— *Being positive about a negative* ——

Saying no takes a great deal of courage, whether you are refusing to do a specific favour, to join a committee, to lend money. . .or anything else you really do not want to do.

Even people who can be quite assertive in other ways may find it difficult to say no. We all want to be liked and there is often a basic fear that, if we refuse someone something they want, they will not like us any more. But if a relationship is built on such fragile foundations that saying 'no' once in a while will cause it to collapse, is it really a good relationship in the first place?

There are bound to be times in your life when you *do* do something simply to please someone else, although it is something you do not really want to do. That is not being submissive; that is simply being a good friend. But if you *always* give in when that person expects you to fall in with their wishes, you need to consider whether you have become submissive – and what has caused you to do so.

Take the case of Roger and Simone. Roger knew that Simone was not happy in large noisy groups of people and so disliked going to parties. When he had to attend a formal function to do with his work, Roger naturally asked Simone to accompany him and, knowing that the occasion was important to him, she agreed. At a later date, Roger asked Simone to come with him when a group of friends were going to a night club disco. This request she felt quite able to refuse, telling Roger that, much as she would like to go out with him, she really did not enjoy the noise and crowded conditions which prevailed at discos. Roger was able to accept the situation, although there are those who might have tried to manipulate Simone into going by making her feel guilty: 'If you loved me you would come with me', 'Go on, do it just for me', or, 'I always do what *you* want'. These are just three of the typical guilt-inducing phrases so often used when one individual is trying to compel another to do something against their wishes.

Being able to say 'no' is an essential part of assertiveness. And there is no need to tell lies or make excuses – as so many people do when trying to avoid doing something. 'I never lend money', is all that is needed – not some long, detailed explanation of how many expenses you have had to face over the last couple of weeks and how you are saving up for a holiday. Or, 'I don't like modern jazz', instead of an invented story of how you have to visit your sick cousin 50 miles away on the day of the concert.

What happens if you don't say 'no'

Suppose guilt does persuade you to agree to something that you do not want to do. Are you going to be happy with yourself? I doubt it. What usually happens is that the person who has given in continues for a while doing what has been asked of them. Then finally they can stand it no longer and – often acrimoniously – make their feelings clear. Not only has that person been unhappy until now but the one who made the original request (and who may not have realised this) will be amazed to be on the receiving end of a vehement outburst. In extreme cases, relationships can be permanently damaged.

If you never reach the point where you can make your feelings clear, you may continue for years doing something you really do not want to do. Even if you do not complain aloud, you are bound to feel angry at the person who got you into this – and even more angry at yourself for not making a stand.

This happened to me in a very trivial way many years ago when I was first married. On my birthday a friend presented me with a box of chocolates of a particular type that I actually dislike. Naturally I did not wish to hurt her feelings by telling her I disliked them, so I accepted them and thanked her very much. If I had stopped there all would have been well. But – and even to this day I am not quite sure why I did it – I went on to tell her the chocolates were, in fact, my favourites. So ever afterwards, on every birthday, Christmas and anniversary, I received yet another box.

I said this example was trivial and of course it was. All I had to do was accept the gift graciously and then give it away to somebody else. But suppose my friend had been giving me something which cost a considerable amount of money or which took a great deal of time and trouble on her part. By pretending in the first place that the gift was particularly welcome, I would be encouraging her to continue. Once involved in that sort of situation, it is very difficult to bring it to an end without both parties feeling awkward and embarrassed. So, I would have eventually have felt extremely guilty about the time or money which was going into something I did not even like.

— 7 —

Not So Happy Families

The one area where we would suppose ourselves able to look for support and trustworthiness – the family – is often the area which induces in us the greatest amount of guilt. The family should be a safe harbour for us to return to after the stormy voyages of life, yet it is often the family itself (or certain members) which causes the worst of those storms.

This is by no means a new phenomenon but only in the last half century have people felt able to discuss their family relationships so openly. Indeed, it has become more and more fashionable to discuss at great length interpersonal relationships within the family.

In some ways this has to be a good thing. How else would those most in need of help and guidance be able to seek it out? But perhaps the tendency has encouraged some people to become too introspective, and to see slights and mistreatment where none was intended. Of course, it is essential for those who are in some way victims to be able to receive assistance and counselling but there is also a danger that some people may come to regard every minor incident of their lives as highly significant and character-scarring.

——— *Parent/child relationships* ———

In most cases the first people with whom the young child has a close relationship is her parents (or those who stand in that position). Initially the child will consider these people to be almost god-like in their knowledge and wisdom. So if, for whatever reason, one or both of these wonderful people does not appear to love her, that child will always assume the fault to be hers, being unable to understand at that point that some people are naturally more able to give and receive love than others.

Even when the child grows into an adult who is capable of understanding that parents are no more likely to be wise and all-knowing individuals than anyone else, it is difficult to shake off feelings of guilt which may by that time have become an intrinsic part of her persona. If your relationship with your parents has caused you to carry around a huge burden of guilt, you are likely to find this quite a difficult concept to face up to.

Unloved and unloving?

The first thing to do in such cases is to acknowledge that your feelings actually exist – and this is not easy. It seems like a betrayal of all that you have been taught if you say that your mother was not kind to you or that you do not love your father. After all, aren't all children supposed to 'love Mummy and Daddy', whether or not Mummy and Daddy actually deserved this most precious of gifts.

In Chapters One and Two we looked at how your self-image is formed at a very early stage in your life. So if, for whatever reason, you felt unloved or rejected by one or both of your parents when you were very young, this feeling will be imprinted on your subconscious mind and remain there unless and until you make a deliberate effort to erase it. No matter how logical and realistic an adult you become, somewhere deep within you there will still be that little girl who felt unloved.

And you will always take the blame for this feeling that you are not loved. The little girl would not have believed that a parent was thoughtless, unkind – or downright bad. She assumed that, if she was not loved, then it must be her fault – she must be unlovable. If you continue to perceive yourself, albeit subconsciously, as an unlovable person, you will automatically seek out those people who will treat you as unlovable – thus reinforcing that inner belief.

Don't despair however. It is possible to come to terms with the reality of the past situation and its effect on your present life. It is not easy but, once achieved, you never have to do it again. You will have changed your inner view of yourself permanently – almost as though you had recorded a new programme over an old audio or video cassette.

———— *Self-help: letter therapy* ————

Because one of the hardest things to do is to admit to yourself that your parent(s) did not love you or that you do not love them, a method which can prove very effective is to write a letter to the parent(s) concerned, one which you have no intention of sending. Sometimes, indeed, the parent has died but, even if they are still alive, no useful purpose would be served by sending them the letter. They are not going to change now, unless they make a conscious decision to do so; you are certainly not going to change them. What you can do is to change your current self-image and thereby their effect on you from this point onwards.

Writing the letter is something you can do for yourself and, because no one in the world but you will ever read it, you can be totally honest. You need not feel that you are being disloyal by writing it, you will not make anyone else unhappy by doing so; you can even destroy it afterwards. So, there should be nothing to prevent you writing from your heart.

Some guidelines

Should you feel that it might help to write such a letter, there are a few guidelines to bear in mind:

- *Begin by addressing it to your parent, using the term you always used:* 'Dear Mummy... Mum... Father... Dad...'.

- *Write whatever comes into your mind* – all those things you have never said. Include also those incidents which may have appeared trivial at the time but which contributed to the feelings about yourself you now have.

- *Don't plan the letter in your mind before you begin.* Structure is unimportant; there is no need to start with the time you were a baby and proceed chronologically through your life.

- *Write as you think.* If, in the middle of a sentence, you feel the need to break off and change the subject, do so. The more spontaneous the letter, the more therapeutic it is likely to be.

- *You do not have to complete it all at one sitting.* Some people prefer to do so, however long the session may take. Others find it easier to spread the process out over several days. Do what feels most natural to you.

What Elaine wrote

Elaine was quite surprised at what she wrote in her letter. She had been adopted at the age of two by a childless couple. The husband was a kind but somewhat weak man, completely dominated by his wife. She was a harsh woman who was incapable of showing any form of love to the little girl and determined to exercise control over her. This she did by any means she considered appropriate: locking the child in the broom cupboard, sending her to bed without food, depriving her of her toys or beating her with a metal-backed hairbrush.

When I first discussed this with Elaine, although she was able to tell me what her life had been like, she found it very difficult to criticise her adoptive mother. 'It was very good of her to take me in,' she said. 'She probably thought she was doing the best for me.' Then, tentatively, 'Perhaps I was a difficult child.'

I explained the letter-writing idea to Elaine and asked her to write one before we met again the following week. I also asked her not to revise, correct or otherwise alter her initial writing as what we really needed to look at were her deep inner thoughts.

Elaine was quite embarrassed when she showed me the letter the following week. In the light of our first meeting, I was not surprised that it began:

Dear Mother,

It was very good of you to take me away from the children's home and into your own home. . .

A little further on, as Elaine began to lose some of her inhibitions, the tone of the letter changed from being somewhat formal to sadly questioning:

'How could you adopt a little girl who needed to be loved and then not love her? Why didn't you love me? Was I so bad?'

The letter continued in this vein for some time, then the writing became less neat and the sentences less well formed:

'You didn't have to hit me. Why the cupboard? So dark. So frightening. I wanted you to love me. I couldn't eat – even when you tried to make me – I was scared to. I hate you . . . I hate you . . . I HATE YOU . . . HATE . . . HATE . . . HATE.'

This, of course, was what Elaine had refused to admit to herself over all the years. She had felt hate for a harsh, cruel woman who had made her life a misery. Now, I am not saying that hate is a fruitful or positive emotion – but it certainly does less harm when expressed in this way than it does if it continues to fester inside. And Elaine was not harming her adoptive mother in any way by writing the letter. In this case, the mother had died some three years earlier but, even had she been alive, the letter would never have been sent so she would not have suffered.

Once Elaine's innermost feelings had been released, she and I went on to talk about the woman who had adopted her, and the problems she must have had in her own early life to cause her to become so bitter and cruel. She became a pitiable creature to the adult Elaine as opposed to the one who had had the power to terrify her as a vulnerable little girl. The letter was destroyed as Elaine would never need to read it again.

Accepting your own feelings

It is extremely difficult to admit that you do not love one or both of your parents, particularly if they are now old or in poor health. But old age does not make saints of sinners. 'You have to forgive him; he's 84 years old', is all very well if age is the only thing making a man difficult. But in some cases he will have been an extremely unpleasant person when he was 24 years old, too.

Even if parents have not been cruel or unkind, you cannot be compelled to love – or even like – them. Perhaps looking back, you can see that they were foolish or ineffectual or simply that your respective personalities were such that you were not able to feel love for them. Love cannot automatically be demanded from a child. I do believe, however, that if you can honestly say to yourself that your parents did their very best for you as they saw it at the time – even if it later turns out that they were mistaken – then you do owe them respect, duty, care and compassion.

Not liking someone who suffers ill health can create feelings of guilt too. When I was first married we had a neighbour who badly suffered from a progressive muscular disease. Because I knew she found walking difficult, if I saw her in the street or at the bus stop I would stop and give her a lift to wherever she was going. I felt sorry for her because of her condition but I could not bring myself to like her: she never had a good word to say about anyone, and was a gossip with a vicious and cruel tongue. And she had been like this long before her illness had been diagnosed.

I found it extremely difficult to criticise someone who was so ill – even to myself. It seemed like kicking someone who was already down. So, knowing that I really did not like this neighbour, I felt extremely guilty about my feelings. It took me a long time to come to terms with the fact that it was all right not to like her as long as I did not let that dislike show itself and add to her problems, and as long as I continued to give her lifts as and when I could.

— *Pregnancy and hostile reactions* —

Pregnancy and childbirth should be joyous times for any woman and yet these, too, can be the source of guilt feelings which may last long after the pregnancy comes to term.

There are, of course, those who never intended to become pregnant in the first place – not least the young girl in her early teens, pregnant perhaps after her first sexual experience. It is easy to think that our world has become so attuned to sex among young people that no one now looks down upon a pregnant teenager, but there are still many such girls who feel that they have let themselves or their families down. One 15-year-old girl I met was distraught not because she was pregnant but because, although her family were being totally supportive, her father had cried when she first broke the news. This was something she had never seen before and she felt extremely guilty for having caused it to happen. (See also Chapter Three.)

There are still members of some religious congregations and certain small communities who manage to make an unmarried, pregnant woman – of whatever age – feel ashamed and guilty. And this feeling probably transmits itself to the unborn child, thus harming two generations.

In his work in the United States, Professor James Eckington showed that, by means of hypnosis, it is possible to regress someone to the time when they were in the womb and show that, although not necessarily able to understand words spoken at that time, the unborn child is certainly aware of atmosphere and emotions which surround it. This is why, when working with pregnant women, I teach them to set aside a particular time to relax in peaceful surroundings and positively communicate good and pleasant thoughts to their unborn child.

If an unborn child is able to absorb the atmosphere surrounding him, it follows that it is harmful for the mother to be obsessed with feelings of shame or guilt. It is even worse if the mother and child are subjected to outbursts of anger or recrimination from those around them.

Elsa's story – left holding the baby

Of course, it is not only very young women who become unintentionally pregnant. Elsa had led an extremely sheltered life, living with her father and three brothers on a farm in mid-Wales. By the age of 37 she had had one or two men friends but no serious romance – and certainly no sexual experience. One summer, an itinerant farm worker came to the area where they lived and struck up a friendship with the family. A natural charmer, he teased and flirted with Elsa and she, lacking experience in such ways, had fallen desperately in love with him. A strong relationship developed between them which Elsa believed would lead to marriage. But at the end of harvest time he left the district as suddenly as he had come and she never heard from him again. Six week after his departure Elsa discovered that she was pregnant.

The atmosphere which surrounded her in the following weeks were negative in the extreme. Elsa herself was ashamed of having (as she saw it) made a fool of herself. Her father was anxious that none of the neighbours in the small, close community should be aware of his daughter's 'shame'. Her brothers, angry on her behalf, would have pursued her lover but nobody knew where he had gone. Eventually, even though this happened in the early 1990s, Elsa was treated like those girls who had found themselves in her position half a century earlier: she was sent away to a relative until after the child was born. She was also told that if she wished to return to the farm – the only home she had ever known – she must first have the child adopted.

Having nowhere else to go and no one to turn to for help, Elsa did have her little daughter adopted, and went back to live on the farm as before. Now she had yet another reason to feel guilty. She condemned herself constantly for having given her child away to strangers and found little reassurance in the knowledge that they were people who would love her daughter and do their very best for her. Elsa felt even worse as she observed the farm animals caring for their young. She told herself that she was not even as good a mother as a sheep or a cow.

Giving a baby up for adoption

There may be many reasons why a woman chooses to give her baby up for adoption but it is always a difficult thing to do. Even if the pressures of the immediate moment will mean that she experiences a sense of relief when the deed is done, the feelings of guilt tend to raise their head at a later date. I have known many women among my patients who have had children adopted – often for the very best of motives and with the baby's best interests in mind – and who, 20 years on, desperately hope for the letter or telephone call which will tell them that their natural child is trying to contact them.

For some women, however, the guilt arises when their child does succeed in tracing them. If a woman has given birth at a very young age and had the child adopted, she may well have gone on to marry and have other children without ever mentioning the first birth. Because all adopted children now have the right to trace their natural parents, there is always the possibility that one day her now adult child will contact her or, worse still, turn up without warning and upset the balance of the life she has now created for herself.

New partners – the right to know

If you have chosen to give up your child for adoption – for whatever combination of reasons – no good purpose will be served if you then surround yourself with guilt for the rest of your life. It certainly will not help the child you have given up. You are also less likely to develop a positive and loving relationship; and any future children will be affected at a subconscious level by your feelings of guilt. The only thing you can do is accept that you took what you considered the best course of action at the time and then turn and face the future, doing your best to ensure that a similar set of circumstances does not arise again. If you succeed, you will have learned from your earlier experience and should be able to assuage the feelings of guilt.

In Chapter Six we looked at the validity or otherwise of telling lies as opposed to making confessions. We saw that it was only safe to tell an untruth (or to fail to tell the truth) if there was no possibility at all of that truth catching up with you at some later time. So, should you decide to enter into a new marriage or permanent relationship, the knowledge that it is now possible for an adopted child to trace its natural mother should convince you that it is better to tell your partner about it at the earliest suitable moment.

If you feel unable to do this, ask yourself why. Are you afraid that he will be angry or will leave you? If so, is this really the type of man you want to spend the rest of your life with? In the final years of the 20th century most people understand that women can and do become pregnant when they are unable to cope with a small child and do, therefore, give these children up for adoption. And no partner has the right to be angry with you for something which happened before you even met. Your partner might well feel he does have the right to be angry, however, if he discovers years later that you have been living a lie all the time that you have been together, by not mentioning to him that you have had a child who has been adopted.

Abortion – and after

Perhaps, having found yourself pregnant and weighed up the situation to the best of your ability, you decided to have an abortion. It is not my place here to condemn or condone abortion in principle; it must be a matter for each individual woman to consider and to do what she feels is best. But even those who truly believe that this was the only realistic course to follow find it difficult to escape feelings of guilt, either at the time or later. These feelings are often increased when you hear or read the views of other people who might have strong moral or ethical objections to abortion – or who have tried in vain to have a child themselves. Because you are already in a vulnerable emotional state, it is easy to be influenced by the opinions of others.

Marriage – and after

Some pregnancy terminations are, of course, spontaneous rather than induced. In other words, the woman suffers a miscarriage – and many such women suffer from tremendous feelings of guilt afterwards. It does not matter how often they are told that there was nothing they could have done to prevent it, there will always be that niggling doubt at the back of their minds; 'Did I overdo things?' 'Was it my fault?' 'Is there something wrong with me?'

For those women who were less than happy to find themselves pregnant in the first place, and then miscarry, these guilt feelings are often even greater.

Tanya – reluctant mother-to-be

Tanya was surprised and angry when she found that she was pregnant. She and her husband Don had always been so careful that she still was not quite sure how it had happened; but happen it had. Tanya loved her husband, was happy in her marriage and had always thought that she would like a family 'one day'. But, at 26 years of age, she was enjoying her life and her career and was not ready to settle down to motherhood.

Tanya and Don discussed the possibility of abortion but neither felt happy with the idea. Gradually, they accepted the idea that they were to be parents – and even began to look forward to it.

Then, just before entering the fifth month of her pregnancy, Tanya suffered a miscarriage. There was no warning, no indication that anything was amiss. Apart from a little morning sickness, she had been well from the very start.

Miscarriage is very difficult for any woman to come to terms with. But Tanya could not help wondering whether she was being punished for not having wanted this baby in the first place. She even asked me whether the baby knew what she was thinking and preferred not to be born rather than to have unwilling parents. I reassured her that this was not so. Even though I am certain that a baby in the later months of pregnancy is aware of the atmosphere and emotions around it, I do not think that such a new foetus would have reached that state of awareness. Even if it had, there are many babies born to mothers who do not really want them, so I could not accept that it was the simplistic matter of choice Tanya feared. In addition, as I reminded her, she and Don had come to look forward happily to the birth of their child so, if the baby was feeling anything at all at that stage it would be pleasure that it was so gladly anticipated.

The after-effects of a miscarriage continue for a long time. However early in the pregnancy it may have been, the mother has suffered a bereavement. Of course the father has been bereaved, too, but at this stage only the mother has been truly close to the child so, no matter how unhappy or sympathetic the father, it is impossible for him to understand just how she feels. One major after-effect is that any subsequent pregnancy will be accompanied by fear rather than joyful anticipation. Even when she has passed the stage at which her earlier miscarriage occurred, the mother is likely to be more than usually anxious about the progress of her unborn child.

The Miscarriage Association

Because women who have suffered miscarriages tend to feel – perhaps rightly – that only others who have been in the same situation can ever understand what they are going through, many of them find help and support from the Miscarriage Association.

Members meet and talk together, help is given by visiting therapists and, in many cases, women who have gone on to successfully give birth to one or more children remain in the group to
give hope and encouragement to newer members. There are
branches of the Miscarriage Association in almost every town
and you will find the address at your local library.

— Difficult pregnancies and bonding —

While some women appear to float through pregnancy in a joyous haze, for others the journey is stressful and uncomfortable.
Fatigue, discomfort, unpleasant symptoms – all these can detract
from what should be a happy time. Feeling this way, the expec-
tant mother begins to question whether she is 'normal', when it
appears to her that every other pregnant woman is coping won-
derfully and feeling on top of the world.

This is even more the case when it comes to labour and childbirth. Even those for whom it comes easily experience a certain
amount of pain and discomfort – and some women are unfortunate enough to have a very difficult time, perhaps ending with a
Caesarian section or a forceps delivery. Is it any wonder that for
many the supposed wonderful surge of maternal feeling when
they first behold their tiny baby never happens? Yet this feeling
of mother-love has been written and spoken about for so many
years that the mother who does not experience it suffers guilt,
believing that she must be 'odd' or different from everyone else.

Having worked extensively with pregnant women, up to and
after the birth itself, I can assure you that not experiencing instant
maternal feelings does not make you at all odd or different. Yes,
some women do have this feeling as soon as their child is born –
but many others do not. And some mothers experience it with the
birth of one child and not with another. There is no hard and fast
rule, and no set time when the special bond between mother and
child is forged.

Olivia's third pregnancy

Olivia already had two children when she became pregnant again. Although she suffered no serious illness, this pregnancy was not a comfortable one. Morning sickness seemed to go on for months, she developed sciatica because the baby was pressing on the sciatic nerve, her blood pressure went up and her hands and feet became swollen. Finally she had to go into hospital for bed-rest some four weeks before the birth was due.

The labour was protracted, and more painful than either of her previous two. When at last her daughter was born, all Olivia wanted to do was sleep. She explained to me later that, when she awoke in bed in the ward and saw her new baby in a crib beside her, she felt absolutely nothing. No surge of maternal love, no feeling of joy – nothing. She would not have hurt the baby in any way but neither did she have any great desire to hold her.

During the days that followed, first in the hospital and later at home, Olivia did all the usual things for her daughter. She fed her, bathed her, changed her and held her – all the time feeling nothing and all the time feeling guilty because of that lack of emotion about which she told no one in case they thought her strange. In fact, it was about six weeks before she experienced a surge of love for her baby but, once that happened, the special bond was forged and was never broken.

If, like Olivia, you have failed to experience a sudden rush of maternal love immediately after the birth of your child, please don't worry that there is anything wrong with you. Instant mother-love is not a universal experience and, particularly if you are physically tired or the birth has been a difficult one, it could take several weeks before you finally bond fully with your baby.

Marital breakdown – what about the children?

Even when they are considerably older, there are many ways in which your children can cause you to feel guilty. Take the situation when you decide to divorce or separate. This is a difficult enough decision for anyone to make, and may bring its own feelings of guilt. Whatever the statistics, there is a tendency to think of yourself as a failure, someone who could not make a marriage work.

Many women tell themselves that they must stay in a marriage 'for the sake of the children'. Yet children of all ages are so sensitive to the atmosphere around them that, even if they have not been told of friction between their parents, they will certainly be aware that something is wrong. They might well guess, wrongly, that they are the cause of all the problems. So, if separation is inevitable, it is better to tell your children as soon as possible.

Of course, it is essential that children of all ages are assured at every stage of a separation that each of their parents still loves them, and that the fact that they will no longer be living together does not change that love. Where possible and appropriate parents should talk to the children together, presenting a calm and united front and explaining the fact of the separation while avoiding blaming or criticising each other. In some cases this is not possible – one parent may have gone off with another partner, for example – but the children still need to be reassured that they are loved and that the separation is in no way their fault.

Because of the sad fact that so many marriages now end in divorce or separation, children today usually cope far better with the situation than they would have done a generation ago. One child, when asked by her mother whether anyone at school had commented on her parents' divorce, said quite calmly, 'Not really. Anyway Gemma's parents have been divorced for years and Trisha's mother lives with another man now.'

—— *Divorce and problem children* ——

It is not unusual for older children to deliberately try to make one or both parents feel guilty – and then to take advantage of that feeling. Mandy was 10 when her parents separated, and she and her 14-year-old sister lived with their mother but spent some weekends and holidays with their father and his new wife. Mandy soon became adept at making the most of this situation. If her mother told her to go to bed or to do her homework, she would threaten to go and live permanently with her father. If her father did not buy her the things she wanted, she said that she would not come to see him any more.

A child who is acting in this way is demonstrating anger and unhappiness at the situation – often because of obvious friction and animosity between the parents. While she cannot be allowed to get away with it, it is up to her parents to give her all the love they can, to refrain from criticising one another and yet be firm with the child and not give in to emotional blackmail.

———— *Bullying or bullied* ————

If you suspect that your child is being bullied, you may have to probe gently to discover the truth – most children become defensive if asked outright. Should you discover that you were right then you *must* tell the school at once. Most teachers are quite used to handling this sort of situation once they know what is going on. This is also a time when you need to be particularly loving and supportive to your child, letting them know that you understand just what they are going through and doing all you can to boost their self-confidence in other areas of life.

We all like to think that our children are pleasant and reasonable and would never do anyone harm. But every adult thug and criminal was once someone's child. It is extremely distressing to learn that your son or daughter is being bullied – but it is also distressing to be informed that your son or daughter is the school bully.

Any reasonable mother who discovers that her child is deliberately doing something wrong – stealing, being violent towards others or towards property, glue-sniffing or taking drugs, for example – is bound to feel guilty. Is it her fault? Did she do something wrong when bringing up the child?

In cases where there really has been a problem during the child's early years and the child is reacting to this trauma – it is usually fairly obvious to the mother and outside professional help should be sought.

—— *Impossible to handle* ——

What about the family with several reasonably-behaved children and just one who is impossible to handle? The mother is still likely to feel guilty, particularly if the child's behaviour is such that other people become aware of it – and perhaps even comment unfavourably.

Should this difficult situation apply to you, there are some points you might wish to consider:

- If you have several children and only one is misbehaving, you may find it difficult to understand because you feel you have always treated them all identically. But, of course, each one is in a unique position. She may be the first born, who, having had the opportunity of being an only child, perhaps resents competition for parental attention. She may be the youngest, with experience of the good and bad side of being the 'baby' of the family. Or she be a middle child, feeling (rightly or wrongly) that everyone else is in a more advantageous position.

- There are some problems about which you must seek outside help. Glue-sniffing can prove fatal, as can the inappropriately named 'joy-riding'. Dabbling with soft drugs can lead to involvement with hard drugs, and with crime in order to finance the habit. Anorexia and bulimia can seriously and permanently damage health and may even be fatal. Such serious problems call for guidance and assistance from those with appropriate experience.

- With behaviourial problems, it is often the case that the child is simply seeking attention and it is a case of 'better to be punished than ignored'. Perhaps you could find a way of giving them more of your time – not simply when difficult issues arise but on a regular basis. Of course time is a commodity which is often hard to come by for many people, but it is well worth making the effort. If the child always seems to want your attention at the most inappropriate moment, acknowledge her, and say that it is not possible to stop what you are doing at this precise instant but you will talk to her as soon as you have completed your present task. It is vital that you keep your word. If the promised moment never comes, the child will lose all faith in you and your promises, and further difficulties could ensue.

- Prevention being better than cure, as soon as they are able to understand you, let your children know that they are important to you in their own right. If they are convinced that they really matter to you and that you will always take their side and help them overcome any difficulties, you may be able to avoid behavioural problems arising later.

— 8 —

Sexual Stresses – and Guilt

Sex is the bread and butter of much of the media. You can read articles telling you how to find it, or gossiping about the sexual antics of people in the public eye. There are pornographic videos and magazines, as well as serious (and pseudo-serious) tomes on the best ways of practising it. And newspapers report all too regularly on the horror and misery of sexual abuse. For anyone who cares to read it, there is also a plentiful supply of erotic fiction, ranging from the mildly titillating through the graphically biological to the downright unbelievable. Even conventional romantic fiction is being spiced up these days.

Sex *can* be a delightful and fulfilling demonstration of love for another person, but it can also cause extremes of guilt. And those who suffer from such guilt often feel unable to discuss their emotions, believing perhaps that everyone else has an idyllic and constantly orgasmic sex life.

——— *Well – what is normal?* ———

Most people would suppose that heterosexual couples, whether married or not, are most likely to have a satisfactory sex life – but

103

this is not necessarily the case. Even within otherwise happy relationships, sex may create problems. Because in this area there is no such thing as 'normal' or 'average', it is quite possible that two people who love each other dearly may have totally different needs and desires.

If one partner feels that he or she would like to have sex every day while the other (while still enjoying it) would like it less frequently, it is usually the latter who feels guilty – believing perhaps that there is something wrong with them. This is even more likely when there is real love between the two. Because of a natural desire to please the person they care for, someone who is less sexually inclined may force themselves to take part in love-making more often than they would really wish. But no one can put on an act of this kind for a prolonged period of time. Unless the couple are able to sit down together and talk about their needs and desires, resentment and dissatisfaction are likely to grow on the part of one or both of them.

It is usually thought that the man is naturally the more anxious of the two for frequent sex but, while this may often be the case, it is by no means always true.

Unequal partners

After two years of marriage, Vanessa and Bill were still very much in love. They were both in their late twenties and extremely career-minded, each doing well within the different organisations they worked for. The only area of conflict within the marriage was their different physical needs. Though they both found sex enjoyable, a problem arose with regard to frequency.

Vanessa was a woman of very strong desires and would have liked Bill to make love to her every night, while he only felt the urge to do so about two or three times a week. When they lay in bed together on the other nights, Bill would dearly have liked to hold his wife in his arms but if he did so she would quickly become aroused and he would either turn away, knowing he was disappointing her, or would (in his words) 'perform' because it was expected of him and he was capable of doing so.

The situation was unsatisfactory for both of them. Bill began to feel inadequate and became anxious that Vanessa might look for someone whose needs would match her own. Vanessa worried that, by being over-demanding, she would lose her husband's love. She was also concerned that she was not 'normal' and began to feel guilty about having such strong desires.

Fortunately for Bill and Vanessa there was sufficient love between them to enable them finally to sit down and discuss the problem. They decided to consult a therapist who specialised in difficulties of this sort (for details see Useful Addresses at the end of this book) and, over a period, were able to create a sex life with which both felt happy.

Kinky sex

Many couples are not so fortunate. In some cases of sexual incompatibility each partner tries to make the other feel that it is her (or his) fault – that s/he is different or odd and should try to change. Just as little children assure parents that 'everyone' is going to have a particular toy for Christmas, those who are sexually disappointed attempt to persuade their partners that 'everyone' does it their way.

This is particularly likely to be the case if one of them has sexual needs which seem to their partner to be 'odd' or 'kinky'. There is nothing wrong in unusual approaches to sex, whether in regard to words, costume, accessories or actions, *provided both partners are happy with it*. Problems arise when one partner does not enjoy the methods the other prefers to use.

Because, where love and affection exists, there is always a solution – even if that solution involves compromise. It is essential that the couple talk together about their problem and then seek professional help if necessary. The trouble is that, even in our so-called 'enlightened' age, many people – particularly women – find it extremely difficult to discuss such intimate matters with their partners, let alone with an outsider. Without discussion, however, there is bound to be frustration on one side and a sense of failure on the other, neither of which is likely to lead to a long and happy relationship.

Sexual betrayal

Even excluding the prevalence of HIV and AIDS, one of the greatest causes of guilt within a relationship is the sexual betrayal by one partner of the other. Whether this takes the form of a series of one-night stands or a prolonged affair – and whether it is the man or the woman who behaves in this way – there is going to be guilt, unhappiness and the probable breakdown of the relationship. Even so-called 'open relationships', where each partner is ostensibly free to indulge in sexual liaisons elsewhere, are unlikely to be long-lasting. When they are, a little probing beneath the surface will often reveal that one partner wishes that the situation was different.

Nadia told me that she and her husband were 'children of the sixties'. They had come together when 'free love' was the order of the day and had carried on with this concept even though they had been married for many years and now had two adult children.

But now Nadia wished things could be different. Her husband still had affairs with other women – none of which lasted for long and none of which (he assured her) affected his love for her or his wish to remain married. He was always careful to practise safe sex and was quite content for his wife to have her 'little adventures', too, if she wished.

But Nadia was tired of the promiscuous life and wanted a quiet and settled relationship with her husband. However, when she tried to discuss this with him, he accused her of reneging on their original agreement. So she felt guilty.

This, of course, is not as common as the type of guilt normally associated with adultery – in which it is the one who is having the extra-marital relationship who feels guilty about betraying their partner. This guilt is usually even more pronounced when the betrayed partner does not even realise what is going on.

It is not uncommon for the one who is having the affair to 'accidentally' leave clues around for their partner to find. There may be two psychological reasons for this:

- The one having the affair would really like to end it but does not know how and is hoping that a confrontation with their partner will bring the matter to a head, enabling them to escape from a situation within which they feel uncomfortable. They may, in addition, feel the need to be punished in some way and think that they are getting away with it too easily.

- The one having the affair would prefer the marriage or long-term relationship to come to an end, thus releasing them to be permanently with the new partner. However, s/he lacks the courage to tell the husband/wife. Then the only solution seems to be to leave clues around so that the husband/wife discovers their betrayal and takes the initiative in bringing the marriage to an end. Such 'clue-dropping' is the action of a person who is basically weak but who may be hiding behind the excuse of not wanting to hurt either party. The fact is, that if s/he truly did not want to cause hurt, the long-term affair would never have been embarked upon.

It is also quite common, when one partner is involved in an adulterous affair, for that partner to do all he or she can to make the other person feel guilty. 'If you had been more loving/less busy with the children/less interested in your career I would not have had to look elsewhere.' If these or similar accusations have been hurled at you, don't allow yourself to feel guilty. You may have been at fault in some way but if so your partner should have told you how he felt, giving you the chance to put your side of the story and to make changes if you chose to do so.

Safe sex and one-night stands

Ever since the mid-1980s, there has been the added problem of AIDS to be considered. If one partner has failed to practise safe sex when having an affair, however brief, there is an additional and valid reason for guilt and anxiety. However certain they may be of the background of that particular partner, they cannot know whom he or she has been with in the past and what *their* history may have been.

Annabel and James had been together for over 10 years. They had many interests in common but also separate hobbies. James was a passionate golfer while Annabel belonged to a local folk music club which she attended once a week. She knew many people there, both men and women, but saw them as friends and was not sexually attracted to any one of them.

One evening there was a party to mark the club's anniversary. Everyone – including Annabel – had rather more to drink than usual. Unused to being drunk, she eventually found herself on the floor of the store room having sex with Rick, a man she had known for some time but never thought of as more than an acquaintance. When she finally made her way home in a taxi, she was relieved to discover that James had not yet returned from a card-playing evening at a friend's house. She had a bath, went to bed and straight to sleep.

Next morning Annabel woke to a horrified realisation of what she had done. She could cope with the morality of the situation by telling herself that this was a one-off and that she had been foolish but there was no need for James (who had never met Rick) ever to know what had happened. The horror was caused by the fact that, the sex having been spontaneous, no form of protection had been used and she did not know anything about Rick or any partners he might have had in the past.

Without saying anything to James, Annabel arranged to have an AIDS test. The doctor told her that, although she could have a test immediately, any infection might not appear for some time and she could not be pronounced clear until she took another test *in six months time.*

Annabel described that long wait as 'six months of hell'. For one thing she had to live with the fear that she might have become infected. For another, she did not dare to have sex with James in case she developed an infection and could pass the virus on to him. If she told James about Rick, she might lose him. If she did not tell him, what excuse could she make for refraining from sexual contact for six months?

Quickly deciding that she could not tell James about Rick, Annabel invented a series of minor illnesses over the ensuing six months. But, although he accepted her explanation in the beginning, James became more and more suspicious that she was deliberately avoiding contact with him. Never suspecting the real reason for her behaviour, he began to think that she no longer loved him or that she was involved with another man.

Fortunately Annabel's second test proved clear and she and James were able to resume their former loving relationship before any permanent harm had been done – although it took some time before James felt completely secure again.

Homosexual and lesbian relationships

In the more enlightened atmosphere of the late 20th century, many people have no qualms about stating their preference for members of the same sex, but to some it is still something to be hidden from other people – and sometimes even from themselves.

It does not matter whether a person is homosexual or heterosexual provided they are happy with what they are. Problems arise when someone tries to *make* themselves act in a way contrary to their inner nature because they think this is the 'right' thing to do. And guilt is often a major influence in such instances – particularly if s/he believes that the family is unable to accept the true situation.

This belief, however, is not always correct. Christopher was terrified of telling his parents that he was homosexual. He thought that his father would disown him while his mother would be greatly distressed. But eventually, he felt he could no longer hide the true situation from them and was completely taken aback by their reactions. Even his father, normally a somewhat strict and straitlaced man, accepted the situation, and Christopher discovered that his mother had guessed some time ago and was just waiting for him to talk about it.

Coming out

Many homosexual men and women only come to accept their true preferences after a period of forced heterosexuality – which often includes marriage or a long-term relationship with a partner of the opposite sex. They then have to face the difficulties involved in telling not only parents but spouses and even children. Some put off doing so for months or even years, thereby heaping upon themselves increased guilt because, if they cannot be true to themselves, how can they possibly be true to others?

In very few such cases do children turn against their parents. Kathy had been married and then divorced when her two sons were still very young. She brought them up alone, and it was only after they had left home to lead lives of their own that she became deeply involved with Ruth. The two women had been close friends for years and now discovered that they wanted a full and close loving relationship. Ruth had no children but Kathy was terrified of telling hers the truth so, in the beginning, she said that she was simply going to share a home with her long-term friend. Eventually she grew upset at having to deceive her sons and, still fearful, explained the true situation.

After their initial surprise, the young men were both loving and supportive. They were pleased that their mother was at last finding happiness. Kathy herself was overjoyed and only regretted the time wasted in keeping her relationship with Ruth secret.

If you have been keeping your sexual preferences secret from those closest to you, you have probably suffered the harmful effects of guilt-related stress. No honest person enjoys living a lie, particularly when that lie involves a betrayal of your innermost feelings. Do at least consider letting those you love know how you feel – especially if you are involved in a 'secret' relationship.

Ask yourself what is likely to happen when you come out. There will probably be initial surprise – even shock in some cases – and certain people may need time to grow accustomed to the idea (although there will probably be some who guessed the truth a long time ago). Once that initial period has passed, anyone who truly cares for you, whether family member or friend, will be pleased for you to be happy. And anyone who cannot accept you for what you are is not really worth bothering about. Whatever the reactions of others, you will lift a great burden from yourself by being honest and open and this, in turn, will release you to go forward and enjoy a loving and fulfilling life.

Sexual abuse of children

Children who have been sexually abused experience many different emotions, not least of these being fear, anxiety, unhappiness and shame. This last emotion is usually induced by the abuser ensuring that the victim tells no one because if s/he does s/he will be considered 'bad', 'wicked' or 'dirty'. The one thing no child victim experiences is anger. Somehow they accept that the blame must be theirs – that they must indeed be bad or these terrible things would not be done to them. Left to fester uncounselled, these feelings become extreme guilt which, in turn, leads to the destruction of the future adult's self-esteem.

This even occurs when the adult has succeeded in blocking from conscious memory the actual incidences of abuse. Nothing is forgotten in the subconscious mind, so the effect is just as devastating whether the individual can recall the events or not. This is where hypnotherapy as practised by a skilled and ethical therapist can be so beneficial, as it is possible to draw from the 'hidden memory bank' any event which as happened in that person's life.

Inducing such recall is not the painful experience you might imagine. However distressing the original incidents were, at the time they took place they were being seen and felt by the eyes and mind of a child who took the blame and was therefore unable to be angry. When looked at later through the eyes of a thinking adult, that adult is aware of the realities of the situation and will become extremely angry on behalf of the child they once were.

The alternative would be far worse. Keeping the past bottled up within you can never be healthy, whereas there are specific techniques a good hypnotherapist can use which will ensure that recalling those lost memories will not re-create in you the pain with which they were initially associated. After all, you are no longer the same person. You are older, with a much greater knowledge of the good and bad abroad in the world. You do not now have the small child's belief that adults know everything and are always right; you know that everyone has strengths and weaknesses and that, sadly, some of these weakness take the form of abuse.

Most children who are sexually abused are also physically hurt – and this hurt is combined with fear and a sense of powerlessness. Physically they do not have the strength to prevent what is happening and, if their abuser is to them a figure of authority, they are also emotionally powerless to refuse. However, in most cases it is the physical pain or bruising which heals more quickly, whereas unless they are helped, the emotional effects can last a lifetime, damaging all future relationships.

Therapy for childhood sexual abuse

Over the past few years, in common with many other therapists and counsellors, I have been approached by more and more women (and some men too) who have been struggling all their adult lives to come to terms with abuse which happened to them in childhood. Perhaps it was the creation of Childline which suddenly made it acceptable to talk about such matters. In practically every case it is possible to help these adults deal with the emotional damage done by past abuse (even those who may have lived as long as 50 years or more with their secret 'guilt'), and to live happier and more peaceful lives.

The betrayal of abuse is magnified when the abuser was the child's own father, the one man whom she ought to be able to trust implicitly. And, if she believes, rightly or wrongly, that her mother was aware of the situation yet did nothing to prevent it, betrayal was heaped upon betrayal.

However much some mothers may shut their eyes to what is happening in their own household, it must be extremely difficult not to suspect what is taking place. As one of my patients, whose mother has been dead for some time, said to me: 'She must have known. Where did she think he was going to when he left her bed after midnight several times a week and didn't return for quite some time?'

Understandably, no woman wants to believe that the man she shares her life with could molest any child – particularly her own. But the guilt which can result from such deliberate self-deception can last a lifetime. Mother and daughter might never mention the subject but each will be aware of the truth. The daughter, as the victim, can be helped to come to terms with the past. For the mother, as the secondary perpetrator, this is seldom possible.

—— *Rape, abuse and harassment* ——

Of course, it is not only children who can be the victims of sexual abuse. Instances of rape and the trauma which results are widely reported in the media – and yet such news probably only touches the tip of this horrendous iceberg. For every case which is reported and followed through, there are many which no one ever hears of.

There may be many reasons for reticence on the part of the women victims. They may feel that they would rather try to forget the incident or to seek private counselling. Some mistakenly feel that they have somehow become unclean and should be ashamed of what happened to them. Many are deterred by the often light sentences handed out to rapists, or the distressing words of some unthinking judges who may try to imply that the woman was somehow 'asking for it'.

Obtaining support

While I fully understand the above reasons for not making official complaints, I do believe that – distressing as the process may be – it is far healthier to allow yourself to become angry and to pursue justice as far as you possibly can, rather than to allow another individual to diminish your self-esteem, or to withdraw from society altogether. And, although I am not in favour of extreme militance, much support at such times can be gained from some of the women's groups which now exist as well as from the Victim Support Agency (see Useful Addresses at the back of this book).

Whether the victim decides to pursue the matter or not, it is vital for her to talk about her ordeal if it is not to do her permanent harm. Some women find that their families or friends are both supportive and sensible, and can give all the help that is needed. But for many it is the trained professional counsellor who is best able to help them regain their confidence – with regard to men in particular and the world around them in general.

However dreadful the abuse of rape may be, the horror must be even greater when the offence was committed by someone you know and formerly trusted, whether he happened to be a steady boyfriend or even a husband. To the fear and indignity suffered in such cases is added the self-criticism of wondering how you could have been so mistaken about another human being. This self-criticism plays a great part in the decreased confidence which generally follows such an attack.

Over the years, I have counselled many women who have been raped or otherwise sexually abused and, whatever their intellect may tell them, almost without exception they feel guilty – that what happened must in some way have been their fault. This is one of the reasons why it is so important to talk about your feelings as, without input from another person, you are unlikely to be able to escape such thoughts and return to living a full and contented life.

Sexual harassment – even when nothing actually takes place – is also a violation of the woman (or man) victim. Smutty remarks, innuendo, over-familiarity, suggestive propositions, any or all of these can constitute sexual harassment and can cause real distress to the victim. Because, particularly in the workplace, the victim is usually much younger and less senior than the perpetrator, she often feels that she is not in a position to do or say anything about it. But there are certain steps you can – and should – take.

- Make it quite clear to the perpetrator that you do not like whatever it is that he is doing and tell him to stop.

- Talk about what has happened to someone you feel will be sympathetic. This will help you to feel better about yourself. You may also find that you are not the only victim, and there is always strength in numbers.

- Keep a written record of the harassment and, if it does not stop, make an official complaint (keeping a copy for yourself). You may choose to complain directly to someone in a senior position or through a personnel officer, or an official of a union if you belong to one.

- Never allow the perpetrator to put the blame on you – as he will often try to do. Perhaps you are very pretty or wear short skirts – but that is no excuse for harassment.

If there is anything in your past or present life which has tarnished sex or personal relationships for you, do seek help because such experiences *can* be overcome, leaving you free once more to get on with your life and enjoy it as you should.

— 9 —

Bereavement – and Regret

How strange it is that the one thing in life we are all going to face at some time is the one thing we are never taught to deal with. No matter who we are or what we do, at some point we will have to cope with the death of someone close to us. Yet no one ever tells us what we may feel at such times or how we are likely to react. So when we do find ourselves confronted by a whole range of emotions, we don't know whether we are reacting normally or whether our feelings are unusual and unwarranted.

Although it is primarily the emotional results of bereavement with which we are dealing here, it is as well to bear in mind that grief can dramatically affect the body too. In *Mind Over Body*, Dr Vernon Coleman refers to recent papers and reports indicating this, and states that one such report '. . .demonstrated that the immune system of a recently bereaved individual shows a marked reduction in efficiency; sadness changes the body's ability to cope with disease.'

— *Emotional stages of bereavement* —

There are three distinct emotional stages to dealing with bereavement. They usually present themselves in the same order to everyone, although some overlapping is involved. These emotions are:

- Grief

- Anger

- Guilt

Any attempt to stifle or deny any or all three is likely to lead to problems at a later date, so let's take a closer look at them.

Grief

It is very natural to feel unhappy, to cry and to be distressed when someone we love or care for dies. And tears should be allowed to flow without any sense of embarrassment. It is all part of the cleansing and healing process.

Once the initial weeping period is over, however, it is as well to sit down and consider just why you are crying. You may be crying for yourself because you have lost someone precious to you, because you are the one left behind, because you are frightened of the future. . . for any number of reasons. There is nothing wrong or unusual about any of these reasons for your tears – but it is important to understand them. You are not really crying for the person who has died.

Of course, particularly if the one who had died was still very young, there is sorrow for the life cut short and for the things she or he will never see or do, but even in that respect the departed has no need of your sadness, and cannot benefit by it in any way.

If you believe that death is the end of everything and there is nothing more to come, then the person who has died no longer

117

exists in any form and therefore cannot be in any pain or distress. If you think that there is something more after this life – whatever you believe that 'something' to be – then the person who has died has progressed to a place where she or he is no longer suffering emotionally or physically. Either way, the lost one has no need of your tears; you shed them for yourself.

You may find as many do that, after the initial grieving period, you no longer cry for the person who has died and yet other things cause you to be tearful. A widow told me that some six months after her husband's death, she no longer wept for him yet found herself becoming tearful at the sound of a particular piece of music or a sad (or even happy) scene on television. This is quite normal; she had reached the halfway stage between extreme grief and becoming healed.

Anger

Some people who have been bereaved are astounded to find just how angry they become with the person who has died. They then feel guilty about their anger – how can they possibly blame someone for leaving them when that someone could do nothing about the departure?

Be assured that anger too is normal. You are not really angry with the person who has died but at the world in general. Because you need a focal point for all this anger, and particularly if it is also tinged with fear about your future, that focal point may be the one you have just lost. How dare they go and leave you to cope all alone!

You are likely to find yourself angry at many other things, and other people, too. When my husband died some years ago at a comparatively young age, I found myself becoming furious when I saw elderly couples arm in arm. It seemed so unfair that they had what I could never have. There were days when my anger was at anything beautiful: the sun for shining, the daffodils for being golden, the sky for being blue. . .life for going on normally.

This angry phase passes but problems arise if you do not expect it and then find yourself having to cope. You begin to wonder if you are 'odd', as sometimes the thoughts you have seem so strange and even unjustified. It *is* a very disturbing experience, but it will pass – as it has for many others before you.

Guilt

There are so many reasons why we feel guilty when someone has died. Some are logical and understandable, and some trivial and unreasonable. Because guilt is one of the main stages of bereavement, if there is no real cause for it, you can be sure we will find one. Diane certainly did:

Diane and the last wish denied

Diane was staying with her 60-year-old mother, who had been suffering for some time from a progressive illness which everyone knew would eventually lead to the breakdown of her immune system and death. But she was not considered to be in imminent danger.

Because of her condition, the mother was on a restricted diet and, wanting to do the best for her, Diane ensured that this diet was rigidly adhered to. One summer evening she gave her mother a small portion of ice cream (all that was allowed) after her meal. When her mother said that she had really enjoyed the ice cream and would love a little more. Diane (with the best of motives) gently but firmly refused.

That night the mother died in her sleep. When other members of the family arrived at the house next day they found a distraught Diane. Apart from her obvious grief, she was consumed with guilt that she had not given her mother the pleasure of another small portion of ice cream on the last night of her life.

Obviously there was no logic to that thought. Diane had simply been doing what she could to prolong her mother's life by helping her to adhere to the prescribed diet. She could have had no knowledge that her mother was about to die and so had done nothing for which she could blame herself. However, since we all need something about which to feel guilty, and because she had

119

been a good and loving daughter, her mind had to find a reason and had fixed on this one small point.

Many people have far greater reasons (real or imagined) for the guilt they feel after a death and it is on these that we shall concentrate in this chapter. But it is essential to understand that we *all* have to go through these three main stages of bereavement if we are to be able to get on with our lives again.

—— *When death was expected* ——

On some occasions the death which occurs will have been expected. There may have been an accident or the existence of a terminal illness. In the latter eventually, sometimes the death will actually seem like a blessed relief, as it frees the individual from extreme pain or the contemplation of a future of progressive deterioration. Most bereaved people can cope with that sort of relief. What is more difficult to cope with is a personal sense of relief.

Sheila's husband Jack had suffered three strokes, the last of which left him confined to a wheelchair and with limited speech. The couple had been married for over 30 years and their children had grown up and left home. Sheila was willing and able to give up work and devote her time to caring for her husband in their own home.

It was, however, an exhausting life. Jack's paralysis meant that Sheila had to fetch and carry everything for him as well as wash, dress and feed him. Communication between them was difficult as Jack had trouble in forming words and sometimes, when Sheila could not understand what he wanted, he would become frustrated and shout – which made him even more incoherent. At other times Sheila would speak to him but could not be sure from his expression whether or not he understood what she was saying.

A blessed release?

One day Jack had a fourth stroke, and this one ended his life. Sheila was naturally distressed at losing her husband, although she was aware that his condition had made him really unhappy and so in some ways she truly believed that he was now better off. What she had not been prepared for was the enormous sense of relief she felt that she had been released from her daily burden of care. She was horrified at the way she felt; it made her see herself as selfish and uncaring. Yet she was unable to dismiss these guilt-inducing thoughts from her mind.

Of course Sheila had no reason to feel guilty. The fact that she was relieved to be freed from the constant work involved in caring for an often difficult, incapacitated person did not mean that she had not loved Jack or that she had wished him dead. Any mother knows that, however much she may love her children, there are days when she would give anything to be free of them and to do what she wants to do. But at least mothers know that their children will grow up and that the longed-for freedom will eventually come. For carers in Sheila's position, however, the only release comes with the death of the sufferer.

'Never speak ill of the dead' syndrome

Sometimes the person who has died was not the good, caring individual they should have been. Sometimes they have deliberately made another person's life a misery – and the effects of this treatment may have continued long after they had any direct contact with their victim. In such instances, just as we do not have to stop loving someone simply because they have died, the fact of their death does not mean we have to love them if they were unpleasant. There is a tendency – the 'never speak ill of the dead' syndrome – to act as though anyone who has died was automatically good, even when this was most definitely not the case.

Patricia's father was a chauvinistic and autocratic man. He behaved quite reasonably towards his two sons but was bullying and aggressive towards his timid wife and his only daughter. As we have already seen, the child who is badly treated by an adult always assumes at the time that the fault is hers (or his). So when her father picked on her, bullied her and punished her for unexplained misdemeanours, Patricia assumed that she deserved such treatment. As an adult she became confused about the reality of the situation. She didn't *think* that she had done anything so wrong – but poor self-esteem convinced her that she must have done or she would not have been so badly treated by the one man she should have been able to trust.

Patricia came to me for counselling and therapy to help her deal with her poor self-image and the problems it caused her. It soon became obvious that much of it was due to her father and his attitude, and although he had died as the result of a road accident a few years earlier, his influence was still very strong. Happily, Patricia worked through her problems very well and developed a new and enhanced self-esteem which enabled her to makes changes in many areas of her life. But while she came to see that her father had been a bully and a tyrant, she still felt guilty that she did not love him – and had never loved him. She wished that there was some way she could understand him so that she could come to terms with his treatment of her. I was, in fact, able to help her with a technique described later in this chapter (see Dealing With Unfinished Business).

—— *Putting your affairs in order* ——

In western civilisations death seems to be such a taboo subject that many people do not even get round to making a will, though this would benefit their loved ones and prevent a great deal of heartache after their demise. Perhaps they feel that even the contemplation of their own death somehow brings the event itself nearer. Naturally we don't want to dwell on the fact and presumably we all hope that it will be in our sleep and at a grand old age. None the less we know that people die every day in accidents or of illness and it seems only sensible to accept this fact, prepare for it in whatever way seems most appropriate and then get on with living. And for any one who has children, failure to make a will is downright irresponsible.

Words unspoken, deeds undone

It is this very avoidance of the thought of death which often prevents us saying the things we really want to say. Even when we know that someone close to us is dying and we would like the opportunity to tell them how much we appreciate them or how much we care for them, we tend to put off speaking the actual words – always intending to say them tomorrow. Then one day it is too late; there are no more tomorrows. The person has gone and we are left with the guilt and remorse which accompany failure to do what we know we should have done.

People talk of 'putting affairs in order' before death. Surely one of the most important aspects of these 'affairs' is to let those closest to you know how you feel. Some people, of course, find it extremely difficult to talk about their innermost feelings, even when they are well, let alone when they are ill. If you know someone like this, try being the first to speak. Let them know that you love them and care about them; this is something anyone would be happy to hear. And even if they find it difficult to respond with similar words, you will know that you have made them feel good about themselves at a time when they need every ounce of positivity they can muster.

If the death is sudden and unexpected, it can be followed by guilty thoughts of so many words unspoken and deeds undone. Perhaps there has been a rift in the relationship which you always intended to repair but never quite got around to doing. Perhaps it is only after the death that you realise how much you cared for the one who has died or understand how much they cared for you.

Perhaps the relationship between you was never as close as it should have been – and now it is too late to do anything about that.

Lisa's story – the best of intentions

Lisa's parents had never been happy about the idea of her moving in with Jason when she was just 19 years old. They did not like the young man and did not think he would be good for their daughter. When making these feelings clear to Lisa, they were not as tactful as they might have been and only succeeded in making her all the more determined to go ahead with her plans. Once they realised that they could not make Lisa change her mind, the sensible thing for them to do would have been to accept the situation and then – should they prove to be right – stand by, ready to be supportive. Unfortunately this was not their attitude and they made it clear that Jason was not welcome in their home at any time. Lisa reacted as any young woman in love would. She said that if her boyfriend could not visit them, she would not do so either. Parents and daughter parted on extremely acrimonious terms.

During the four years that the relationship lasted, Lisa had no contact at all with her parents. Matters were not made any easier when they proved to have been right about Jason, whose treatment of Lisa grew worse and worse, culminating in a drunken physical attack which left her bruised and frightened. The couple split up and Lisa – feeling that she could not contact her parents at such a time – moved to another part of the country.

As time went by, Lisa's life improved. She got a good job, met a kind and gentle man with whom she fell in love and later married. When their first child was born, Lisa decided to contact her parents to let them know they had a grandson. She got as far as dialling the number but, when she heard her mother's voice, all the old feelings of rejection returned and she put the phone down without speaking. The following Christmas she sent them a card, bearing her address and signed 'from Lisa, Don and Tony' – thereby making her current situation obvious. She waited for some sort of response but, when none was forthcoming, decided that she was not going to give them another opportunity to reject her.

Years passed, and Lisa and Don now had three children. As they grew up and she found herself wanting only the best for them, Lisa began to understand her parents a little better. She still did not think they had acted correctly but at least she realised that their motives had been of the best. From time to time she thought about contacting them but, after the failure of her earlier attempt, she always postponed actual action.

One day Lisa received a letter from her mother saying that her father had died in hospital, and asking to see her. Lisa went immediately and, although the first meeting was awkward and stilted, soon began to forge a new relationship with her mother. When the time came to discuss the original rift between them, each was more able to see the other's point of view and her mother assured Lisa that her father had always loved her and had spoken of her often over the years.

Naturally, Lisa was happy to have found her mother again and for her children to get to know their grandmother. But it was too late now to make things up with her father.

Lisa still suffers from guilt because she allowed her father to end his life thinking that she did not care about him. What hurts her most is that she often thought of doing something about it but never got round to it until it was too late.

Fortunately, there is a very effective method for dealing with such unfinished business with someone who has died.

— Dealing with unfinished business —

The technique described here can help you to say all those things which were never said when the person concerned was alive. It can also help you, by the use of your subconscious, to understand a little more about the attitudes and behaviour of the person who has died.

There are three principal stages:

1 Relaxation – to enable you to access your subconscious mind.

2 Visualisation – positive use of your imagination in order to create a mental picture of the person as s/he was when alive.

3 Use of the subconscious mind to enable you to have a mental conversation with that person and to know intuitively what his or her responses would have been.

Relaxation

You may use any technique with which you are familiar but, if this is an area which is new to you, the following method will be effective:

- Sit or lie comfortably is a place where you will be undisturbed. Close your eyes.

- Starting with your feet and working upwards, tense and relax each set of muscles in turn. Finish with those around the neck and the jaw.

- Spend a few moments concentrating on breathing slowly and evenly, becoming aware of the steady rhythm of your breathing.

Visualisation

Allow a picture to build up in your mind of the person who has died as s/he was at some stage in your lives when you were able to communicate. (If, through illness, or extreme age, they were not fully aware towards the end of their life, you may have to revert to an earlier time.)

Using the subconscious

Here you need to employ a combination of your intuition and your imagination. If you are sufficiently relaxed, you will find this quite easy to do.

- Address the person you are picturing and say to him or her whatever it is that you feel you never had time to say when s/he was alive. (You may do this by speaking aloud or you may prefer to simply think through the conversation in your head.)

- If all you need to do is to tell him or her something without the necessity of a response – perhaps that you wish you had been more patient or more demonstrative – make sure you observe the image you have created so that you are aware of his or her expression as you 'say' the words. The pleasure exhibited will be real and you will know that you have at last had a chance to say what you wanted.

- If you feel the need to ask them questions, such as why they behaved as they did or what they really felt, do this and then allow your subconscious mind to come up with the answer. You may find this difficult to do at first as the tendency is to 'force' the response that your logical mind presents you with. This is not right, however, and you should merely ask the question and then wait. If you are sufficiently relaxed, the correct answer will present itself – and you may well be surprised at what you discover.

You can repeat this process as often as you need in order to free yourself of the feelings of guilt and to be content that you have uncovered all the answers to your questions.

Suicide

If any type of death is going to induce a sense of guilt in those left behind, it must be a death by suicide. To think that someone you knew and loved had reached such a depth of despair and unhappiness, and that you were not aware of it or able to prevent it, is a particular agony.

Some years ago a close friend of mine committed suicide. I had spoken to him on the telephone only a few days earlier and had detected nothing out of the ordinary in his words or voice, and for weeks I wondered how this could be. I asked myself again and again why I did not realise that he was so unhappy and whether I could have done anything to make him change his mind. But the agony I felt can have been nothing when compared to his own family who did not – and still do not – understand how their beloved son, uncle and brother could have reached such depths of despair while they remained totally unaware.

Whatever you may feel – and whatever the legal and religious tenets involved – the fact remains that, if an adult decides to hide from you the fact of their unhappiness and their intention to end their own life, there is nothing at all you can do. Because I believe in reincarnation, and that, if you do not cope with a particular set of problems in this lifetime but decide to end it all, you will have to come back and face that same set of problems in another life, I cannot see that suicide can ever be the answer. But I am looking at the situation through the eyes of someone who is not in the depths of despair and who is enjoying her life – so how can I hope to understand what is going on in the mind of someone contemplating suicide?

The only consolation to be found in a deliberately self-induced death is that, if the person was in such mental torment that this seemed to be the only answer, at least he or she is free of that torment now.

Death of a child

One of the hardest deaths to bear must be the death of a child, and the mother almost always experiences some sensations of guilt. If it is a cot death, an illness or an accident, she will torment herself by wondering constantly whether it was her fault – should she have done something differently or should she have been aware of what was happening?

Even once she has come to terms with the death itself and has realised that she was in no way to blame, she may find it difficult to accept that it is permissible to laugh again and to find joy with any other children she may already have. Should she go on to have another child, she may wonder whether she is trying to replace the one she has lost – and this may make her feel as disloyal as the widow who remarries.

It is the fact that there are so few child mortalities compared with a couple of generations ago that induces such feelings. In our great-grandparents' time, when there was less medical knowledge and sometimes extreme poverty, it was not unusual to hear someone say that she had 'borne eight (or more) children and raised five' and be proud of that fact. But now, when the majority of children survive to become adults, there is a tendency to feel that it must be your fault if one of yours does not.

Any bereaved person can derive great benefit from professional counselling and nowhere is this more true than in the case of a bereaved mother. If you have the misfortune to fall into this category and you find after, say, six months that you are no closer to coming to terms with what has happened, do consider seeking such help. It may well prevent you damaging your own life and that of those closest to you.

Mourning – and children's reaction to death

Whether or not you are religious, there is often great comfort to be found in the ritual which follows a death. For many people, following the traditional routines of their own culture helps to put the death in perspective. This even applics to the death of pets, which is why those who bury their loved cats, dogs, hamsters or budgies will usually pick a few flowers to place on the grave. It is not for the sake of the animal but to help *them* come to terms with the loss that they do so, whether or not they realise this to be the case.

For no one is this sort of ritual more important than for a child. Although they, too, will be unhappy if someone close to them has died, children can be extraordinarily matter-of-fact when dealing with death. Problems arise, however, when adults, acting from the kindest of motives, try to shield the child too much from what is happening.

Celia was very concerned about young Tommy when his grandmother died. She had lived only a few minutes walk away and Tommy had seen her regularly throughout the five years of his life. Not wanting the child to be involved in the funeral or the grieving – and thinking she was doing the best for him – Celia arranged for him to go and stay with friends until the whole thing was over. The result was that, when he came home, Tommy found it difficult to understand how his grandmother could now be 'nowhere' and it took him much longer to come to terms with the loss than it would have done had the matter been explained to him in simple terms in the first place.

You have to be careful of the language you use when talking about death to a young child. So many of the euphemisms we use can cause emotional difficulties later. 'Gone to be with Jesus' can bring about a fear of going to church in case, as one four-year-old put it: '. . .it's full of dead people.' Even more unfortunate can be any link between the ideas of death and sleep, and the difference needs to be clearly explained.

Lucie was six when her auntie died and, in accordance with the family's religious belief and custom, the coffin was brought to the house so that all the family could pay their final respects. To Lucie it seemed that Auntie Meg was fast asleep and, because no one realised what she was thinking, nothing was said to dispel this belief. After her aunt's funeral Lucie began to have nightmares and would wake screaming from her dreams. In her young mind she had come to believe that, should she fall asleep for any length of time, someone would come and bury her.

Death is a part of life and, if we can be sensitively taught to accept this from a very early age, we are far less likely to suffer the frequently accompanying guilt in later years. Even quite a young child will accept the actual word 'dead', provided the adult explaining the situation is sufficiently gentle and sensitive while talking about it. The really important thing, as in matters of sex, is to tell children as much as you think they can understand, according to their age, and then to answer their questions honestly as and when they arise.

—— *Putting grief behind you* ——

However much you may have loved the person who has died, the time will come when you will once again laugh and be happy – and this is just as it should be. You would not want those you love to be unhappy for the rest of their lives should you pre-decease them. In the same way, your lost loved one would not wish you to lead a life of continuous misery just because they are no longer there to share it with you. All human beings are very resilient; they can learn to put the extremes of grief behind them and go on to lead happy and fulfilling lives, even though this does not prevent many of them from feeling extremely guilty when they find themselves beginning to do so.

Even if the person who died was extremely close to you – a

husband, partner, beloved parent or child – eventually you will find things to enjoy in life again. This does not mean that you are less unhappy about losing them nor does it diminish the love you felt (and still feel) for them, so you should not feel guilty. In the beginning, you are likely to find yourself thinking about them all the time but gradually you will go for longer and longer spells without doing so. This is your internal self-protection process in action. No one could exist in an eternal state of extreme grief.

The first few weeks are obviously the most distressing but the first year will probably bring many poignant reminders. Every 'special' day – their birthday, Christmas, Valentine's Day, Mother's Day, anniversaries, and so on – will cause some sadness. Once you have lived through that first year, however, it will never be as bad again.

If people feel uneasily guilty about laughing or enjoying life again after a bereavement, many feel even more guilty when, having lost a husband or partner, they enter into a new loving relationship. If this is your 'guilt', be assured that it is not in any way a betrayal of the love you once shared with the person who has died. If anything, it is a compliment to that love that you feel able to find it again in someone else.

In conclusion

If *you* have been troubled by feelings of guilt in any of the areas covered in these pages – whether or not you were aware that this was the cause of the negativity you have been experiencing – you now have at your fingertips guidelines which will help you to understand the initial causes of the emotion and to work towards overcoming it. By working through the appropriate techniques described, it is possible to alter your self-image and therefore make changes in yourself which will enable you to enjoy a more positive and fulfilling life. Take courage from the fact that you are by no means alone – and start on your self-therapy today.

Additional Reading

Awaken the giant within by Anthony Robbins
How to take control of your mental, emotional and physical
destiny
(Simon & Schuster, 1992)

Be your own best friend by Louis Proto
How to achieve greater self-esteem, health and happiness
(Piatkus, 1993)

Elements of visualisation by Ursula Markham
How to use your imagination in a creative and positive way to
change your life
(Element Books, 1989)

Feel the fear and do it anyway by Susan Jeffers
How to turn your fear and indecision into confidence and action
(Arrow Books, 1991)

The magic power of self-image psychology
by Dr Maxwell Maltz

Living with change by Ursula Markham
Positive Techniques for transforming your life
(Element Books, 1993)

Mind over body by Dr Vernon Coleman
(Guild Publishing, 1989)

Open the window by Joan Gibson
Practical ideas for the lonely and depressed
(Gateway Books, 1985)

Positive thinking by Vera Peiffer

Psycho-cybernetics by Dr Maxwell Maltz

Super confidence by Gael Lindenfield
The woman's guide to getting what you want out of life
(Thorsons, 1989)

Tactics for changing your life by Antony Kidman
Ways to change your thinking habits
(Kogan Page, 1986)

Total confidence by Philippa Davies
The complete guide to self-assurance and personal success
(Piatkus, 1994)

Women under pressure by Ursula Markham
A practical guide for today's woman
(Element Books, 1990)

You just don't understand by Deborah Tannen
Women and men in conversation
(Virago, 1992)

Useful Addresses

Many of these organisations have limited funds so please enclose a stamped, self-addressed envelope with any inquiry.

To find the name of a qualified counsellor in your area:
The British Association for Counselling
1 Regent Place
Rugby, Warwickshire
CV21 2PJ

To find the name of a qualified hypnotherapist:
The Hypnothink Foundation
PO Box 66
Gloucester
GL2 9YG

The National Council of Psychotherapists'
    Hypnotherapy Register
The Secretary,
24 Rickmansworth Road
Watford, Herts,
WD1 7HT

Marriage or Partnership guidance:
Relate (formerly the Marriage Guidance Council)
Herbert Gray College
Little Church Street
Rugby
CV21 3AP

The British Association for Counselling
1 Regent Place
Rugby, Warwickshire
CV21 2PJ

The Brook Advisory Centres (advice for under-25s)
Head Office:
233 Tottenham Court Road,
London,
W1P 9AE

Health
Women's Health Concern
83 Earl's Court Road,
London
W8 6EF

Miscarriage Association (Head Office)
18 Stoneybrook Close
West Bretton
Wakefield, West Yorkshire
WF4 4TP

Women's Alcohol Centre
254 St Paul's Road
London N1 2LJ

Bereavement support
Cruse (Bereavement Counselling)
Cruse House, 126 Sheen Road
Richmond, Surrey
TW9 1UR

SOBS (Survivors of Bereavement by Suicide)
c/o Alison Middleton
82 Arcon Drive
Anlaby Road
Hull, East Yorkshire
HU4 6AD

Rape Victims
London Rape Crisis Centre
PO Box 69
London WC1X 9NJ

General
Relaxation and self-help cassettes are available from:
The Hypnothink Foundation
PO Box 66
Gloucester
GL2 9YG

Self-help groups:
For details of these in your own area, contact the public library,
Citizens Advice Bureau or local telephone directory

Index

PIATKUS BOOKS

If you have enjoyed reading this book, you may like to read other titles published by Piatkus. These include:

Popular Psychology

Adult Children of Divorce: How to Achieve Happier Relationships Dr Edward W Beal and Gloria Hochman

At My Father's Wedding: Reclaiming Our True Masculinity John Lee

Children of Alcoholics: How a Parent's Drinking Can Affect Your Life David Stafford

The Chosen Child Syndrome: What to Do When a Parent's Love Rules Your Life Dr Patricia Love and Jo Robinson

Codependents' Guide to the Twelve Steps: How to Understand and Follow a Recovery Programme Melody Beattie

Co-Dependency: How to Break Free and Live Your Own Life Liz Hodgkinson

Creating Love: The Next Stage of Growth John Bradshaw

Dare to Connect: How to Create Confidence, Trust and Loving Relationships Dr Susan Jeffers

Don't Call It Love: Recovery from Sexual Addiction Patrick Carnes

The Father-Daughter Dance: Insight, Inspiration and Understanding for Every Woman and Her Father Barbara Goulter and Joan Minninger

Fire in the Belly: On Being a Man Sam Keen

Growing Old Disgracefully: New Ideas for Getting the Most Out of Life The Hen Co-op

He Says, She Says: Closing the Communication Gap Between the Sexes Dr Lilian Glass

Homecoming: Reclaiming and Championing Your Inner Child John Bradshaw

Inward Bound: Exploring the Geography of Your Emotions Sam Keen

Marrying an Older Man Maggie Jones

Obsessive Love: How to Free Your Emotions and Live Again Liz Hodgkinson

Off the Hook: How to Break Free from Addiction and Enjoy a New Way of Life Corinne Sweet

Opening Our Hearts to Men: Taking Charge of Our Lives and Creating a Love that Works Dr Susan Jeffers

The Passion Paradox: What to Do When One Person Loves More than the Other Dr Dean C. Delis and Cassandra Phillips
The Right to Be Yourself: A Woman's Guide to Assertiveness and Confidence Tobe Aleksander
Total Confidence: The Complete Guide to Self-Assurance and Personal Success Philippa Davies
When Food Is Love: Exploring the Relationship Between Eating and Intimacy Geneen Roth

For a free brochure with further information on our full range of titles, please write to:

Piatkus Books
Freepost 7 (WD4505)
London W1E 4EZ

TOTAL CONFIDENCE
by Philippa Davies

Confidence is that priceless quality which helps us to live our lives to the full, rather than as mere shadows of what we might be. Using psychological principles and easy-to-follow exercises, *Total Confidence* gives detailed guidelines on how to build your self-confidence. It explores three different areas:

- Thinking with confidence – Learn how to believe in yourself and know yourself better
- Speaking with confidence – Discover how to assert confidence and build more fulfilling relationships
- Projecting confidence – Find out how to convey professionalism and inspire and encourage others

Philippa Davies runs her own business, Voiceworks, which trains top business executives, TV newsreaders and presenters and the general public in communication and presentation skills. She is the author of *Your Total Image* and *Personal Power* (Piatkus).

BE YOUR OWN BEST FRIEND
by Louis Proto

The best route to happiness is to learn how to feel good about yourself and increase your self-esteem. This book shows you how to love yourself unconditionally, for who you are.

- Learn how to use affirmations, visualisations and meditation techniques to enrich your life
- Find out how to nourish yourself better, from within and without
- Discover how love can heal
- Learn how to take responsibility and not be a victim
- Find out how to accept yourself, 'warts and all'

Louis Proto is a well-known author, and was for many years a counsellor and holistic therapist.

DARE TO CONNECT
by Susan Jeffers

Dare to Connect is for everyone who has ever asked:

- Why do I feel so nervous when I walk into a room full of strangers?
- Why do I feel lonely, even though I'm surrounded by people?
- Why do I feel so alienated from my husband/wife/lover?
- How can I pick up the phone and make that important call without feeling anxious?

We all want to be liked or loved and to feel close to our partners, friends and colleagues. What we don't always know is how to make the connection. In this empowering book, Susan Jeffers gives us the insights and tools we need to end our loneliness and create a sense of belonging everywhere we go.

Susan Jeffers has a doctorate in psychology and is a noted public speaker and workshop leader. Her books on fear, relationships and personal growth have been international bestsellers.

HOMECOMING: RECLAIMING AND CHAMPIONING YOUR INNER CHILD
by John Bradshaw

John Bradshaw is a major figure in the field of recovery and dysfunctional families. His 'inner child' work is a powerful, new therapeutic tool. The people who come to his workshops bring with them persistent problems such as addiction, depression, troubled relationships and chronic dissatisfaction. He helps them to reach back to the source of their problems – their childhood and adolescence – and understand how the wounds received then can continue to contaminate their adult lives. He offers them the chance to reclaim and nurture their 'inner child' and grow up again. This experience has transformed their lives. Reading this book will help you to transform your life and find a new joy and energy in living.

HYPNOSIS REGRESSION THERAPY –
AND HOW IT CAN HELP YOU
by Ursula Markham

Hypnosis Regression Therapy – and How It Can Help You answers the questions you may have concerning this increasingly popular therapy. Discover:

- What hypnosis regression therapy is
- How it works
- When it can be used
- If it's right for you

Ursula Markham is one of Britain's most respected hypnotherapists. With the aid of case histories she looks at the problems – such as anxiety, low self-esteem, phobias, depression, impotence, weight, stammering – that can be successfully overcome and shows you how you too can benefit.

THE POWER OF YOUR DREAMS
by Soozi Holbeche

The Power of Your Dreams is based on Soozi Holbeche's experiences of dream work and is an extraordinary guide to our powerful inner world. Using dozens of examples from her own dreams and from her therapy sessions, Soozi explains how our dreams have the power to prophesy, heal, warn, empower and guide. Discover how to:

- Use dreams as a pathway to the unconscious
- Incubate dreams and ask for help and insight
- Recall your dreams and interpret them
- Use dreams to make positive and healing changes in your life

Soozi Holbeche is a dream therapist and healer. Her previous book, *The Power of Gems and Crystals,* has become a bestseller in its field.